Ninja Foodi Grill Cookbook

550 Easy & Delicious Indoor Grilling and Air Frying Recipes for

Beginners and Advanced Users

Kamilia Boutwell

Table of Contents

Introduction

What is the Ninja Foodi Grill?

The Ninja Food Grill is an indoor electric grill! With virtually no smoke, all of your favorite dishes can be grilled, roasted, and air fried!

It's hard to make room for single-purpose countertop appliances, even in the most organized and spacious kitchens. So often, you're going to use a commodity a few times to relegate the cumbersome one-trick pony to the wardrobe, the attic, or even the tag sale. But items that can do more than one thing, and do them well, on your countertop might be worth giving a permanent home.

The newest device is crying out for space? The Ninja Foodi Grill, one of the most recent additions to a growing Foodi products ecosystem. It may also air fry, bake, roast, and dehydrate, in addition to grilling. Here's the lowdown on whether one of our favorite indoor grills is worth the big bucks it's currently selling for — or whether you'd be better off with another.

The Benefits of The Ninja Foodi Grill

The Ninja Foodi Grill. The grill that sears, sizzles, and air fry crisps. Indoor grill and air fryer

500F air circulates around food for amazing surround searing while the 500F high density grill grate creates char grilled marks and flavors, for food that's perfectly cooked on the inside and char grilled on every side with cyclonic grilling technology

With the BTU cooking power of an outdoor grill, it brings outdoor grill flavors conveniently to your countertop any day of the year

Forgot to defrost dinner - Transform foods from frozen to perfectly char grilled in 25 minutes. Dishwasher safe components

Air fry crisp with up to 75 percent less fat than deep frying (tested against hand cut, deep fried french fries), using the included 4 quart crisper basket

What Can Ninja Foodi Grill Do?

As you might expect, they can grill this Foodi. Though it cooks with the lid closed, the lid doesn't press down on food. It is just brand grill marks on one side at a time — if you want a Panini, you'll have to turn it over halfway through cooking. The grate leaves curved grill marks on meats, rather than straight lines.

Apart from grilling, the Ninja Food Grill will air fry, roast, bake, and dehydrate, which overlaps with many of the Ninja Foodi Pressure Cooker and Ninja Foodi Oven features.

Grill

It cooks both fresh and frozen hamburgers, chicken breasts, salmon, and New York strip steaks to test the grilling function — and we were extremely impressed. The chicken and burgers looked like an outdoor barbecue made them. The salmon's skin was delightfully crisp, and the top browned well, even without flipping.

Although the strip steaks did not compare with those outdoor grilled steaks, they turned out better than other steaks in an oven. Although the grilling time was around eight minutes for preheating, the food was easily cooked once on.

Frying Climate

The Foodi Grill competes with the best air fryers we've reviewed. Both fresh and frozen fries came out near those fast-food fries that we find so irresistible to all. While frying, you take out a basket on most air fryers to twist and turn food, so it can be uncomfortable to keep the basket when working. But as the Ninja's lid opens upwards, we found that accessing items that need to be flipped in the crisper basket is very simple.

Baker

You can even bake a cake in the Ninja Foodi Grill in a pinch because the cooking pot is large enough to accommodate an 8-inch pan. Don't expect picture-perfect results, though. A uniformly browned yellow cake came out with a moist tender crumb, but it was badly domed and cracked on top.

This grill might be a fast way to get a homemade dessert on the table if you don't have a full-size oven at your disposal and aren't too fussy about how your baked goods look.

Dehydrated

I was pleased by how well the Foodi Grill dehydrated; finding out the apple rings in seven hours was the ideal degree of chewiness. However, at one time, you can only fit about 18 slices onto the Foodi, which yields about one cup and a half of dried apple rings.

If you love the concept of producing your own dried fruit, even in small quantities, and can keep an appliance running all day or overnight, you'll be satisfied with the outcome.

Roasting

You can roast a small cut of meat on the Ninja Grill if you don't like turning your oven on. A soft, juicy, pork-loin roast came out with a crackling crust.

Tricks to Make Cooking Mistakes Avoid

There are plenty of things to remember, and many common errors to prevent to achieve a perfect Ninja Foodi grill steak. As a beginner, understanding what these grilling errors are, and how to avoid them, is critical. This way, you're on the right track to becoming a grilling pro in no time!

Here are the most common grilling errors starters can avoid:

Uses bad resources

Some of the most common myths about the Ninja Foodi grill are that to achieve delicious and perfectly cooked grilled dishes; you need fancy, expensive tools, and equipment. Despite this, many grillers make the mistake of either using needless or bad instruments. Save your money: You only need a few simple yet reliable tools to get the job done like a long-lasting pair of tongs, a spatula, heat-resistant gloves, a food thermometer, and some clean towels. Often opt for arm and hand safety with the long-handled variety of the tongs and spatula.

Meat thermometer not used

One of the most common Ninja Foodi grill errors is to forego the food thermometer, which often leads to a grilled dish that is either overcooked or undercooked. You don't want visitors to get or see raw or burnt food, so be sure to invest in a decent thermometer to make it easier to read the internal temperatures. Don't worry; you'll know when the food is ready by looking at it once you get the hang of grilling. Meanwhile, get a decent quality food thermometer for yourself.

Too much sauce too soon

There are plenty of grillers making the mistake of slathering the meat with sauce while cooking on the grill of Ninja Foodi. Most glazes, marinades, and sauces contain sugar that easily burns out. Because of this, it will burn your steak on the outside but still raw on the inside. If you want to cook your food evenly, add the right amount of sauce at the end of the grilling process approximately 10 minutes before your food is ready.

No time taken to prepare

Are you aware that every successful cook's rule number 1 is "mis en place," which means all in place? It ensures that everything should be prepare before beginning the cooking process accordingly. The same goes for grilling on Ninja Foodi. Most grillers make the mistake of preparing certain ingredients while on the grill; this contributes to burning or uneven cooking. It is of utmost importance that all of your ingredients are ready. Once you light up, your grill-meat should be thawed and marinated, fruits and vegetables should be diced, sliced or peeled, and sauces mixed.

Holding a dirty grill

Probably the most common grilling error is holding a dirty grill. Not regularly cleaning your Ninja Foodi grill is not only unhygienic but also increases the risk of hazards to your safety. Grease quickly builds up in your grill after just a few uses, which is the number one cause of flare-ups. Also, food can stick more easily to dirty grates that could lead to uneven cooking. If you can to prevent hazards, clean your grill after every use.

Care & Cleaning Your Ninja Foodi Grill

It might appear very tricky to thoroughly clean the Ninja Foodi Grill, but it is not complicated at all. You merely need to follow certain easy steps, and your device is ready to go for another round. It is recommended to thoroughly clean the Ninja Foodi Grill after every use. To clean the unit thoroughly and safely, follow the following guidelines:

- Let the device cool down before cleaning.
- Unplug the device from the power source.
- For quick cooling, keep the hood of the device open.

- The grill gate, splatter shield, crisper basket, cooking pot, cleaning brush, and the rest of the accessories are certified as **DISHWASHER SAFE**.
- The thermometer is not dishwasher safe.
- Rinse the accessories like splatter shield, grill gate, etc. for better cleaning results.
- Use the cleaning brush included with the device for handwashing.
- For cleaning baked-on cheese or sauces, utilize the other end of the cleaning brush for being used as a scrapper for effective hand washing.
- Either towel-dry or air-dry all the components after hand washing.
- **DO NOT** dip the main unit in any liquid, including water.
- **DO NOT** use any rasping cleaners or tools.
- **NEVER** use any sort of liquid cleaning solution near or on the thermometer.
- Always use a cotton swab or compressed air to avoid any damage to the jack.

In case of any grease or food residue left and stuck on the components of the Ninja Foodi Grill, follow the following cleaning steps thoroughly:

1. If the residue is stuck on the splatter shield, grill gate, or any other accessory or part, soak it in warm soapy water solution before cleaning.
2. The splatter should be cleaned thoroughly after every use. For better cleansing, soak it in warm water overnight will assists efficiently in softening the stuck grease or sauces.
3. You can also deep clean the splatter shield by thoroughly immersing it in water and further boiling it for approximately 10 minutes.
4. Moreover, you can then rinse it effectively with room temperature water and let it dry properly for better results.

For deep cleaning the thermometer, you can soak both the silicone grip and the stainless-steel tip in a container full of warm water. But, keep in mind that the jack or the cord **SHOULD NOT** be immersed or soaked in any solution, including water, as mentioned earlier. The thermometer holder of the Ninja Foodi Grill is clearly **HANDWASH** only.

Chapter 1: Breakfast Recipes

Grilled Up Maple Flavored Broccoli

Prep Time: 5-10 minutes
Cooking Time: 10 minutes
Servings: 4

Ingredients:

- 2 heads broccoli, cut into florets
- 4 tablespoons soy sauce
- 2 tablespoons canola oil
- 4 tablespoons balsamic vinegar
- 2 teaspoons maple syrup
- Red pepper flakes and sesame seeds for garnish

Directions:

1. Take a mixing bowl and add soy sauce, balsamic vinegar, oil, maple syrup and whisk well
2. Add broccoli and let it sit
3. Take your Ninja Foodi Grill and press "GRILL" and set to "MAX" mode, set the timer to 10 minutes
4. Let it preheat
5. Once you hear the beat, add broccoli over the grill grate
6. Lock lid and cook until the timer reads zero
7. Serve and enjoy with a topping of pepper flakes and sesame seeds

Nutritional Values (Per Serving):

- Calories: 141
- Fat: 7 g
- Saturated Fat: 1 g
- Carbohydrates: 14 g
- Fiber: 4 g
- Sodium: 853 mg
- Protein: 4 g

Plate-O-Bagels

Prep Time:5-10 minutes
Cooking Time: 8 minutes
Servings: 4

Ingredients:

- 1 cup fine sugar
- 2 tablespoons black coffee, prepared and cooled down
- 4 bagels, halved
- ¼ cup of coconut milk
- 2 tablespoons coconut flakes

Directions:

1. Take your Ninja Foodi Grill and open lid, arrange grill grate and close top
2. Preheat Ninja Foodi by pressing the "GRILL" option and setting it to "MEDIUM" and timer to 8 minutes
3. let it preheat until you hear a beep
4. Arrange bagels over grill grate, lock lid and cook for 2 minutes, flip sausages and cook for 2 minutes more
5. Grill remaining Bagels similarly
6. Take a mixing bowl and mix remaining ingredients, pour the sauce over grilled bagels
7. Serve and enjoy!

Nutritional Values (Per Serving):

- Calories: 300
- Fat: 23 g
- Saturated Fat: 12 g
- Carbohydrates: 42 g
- Fiber: 4 g
- Sodium: 340 mg
- Protein: 18 g

Creative Potato Pancakes

Prep Time: 10 minutes
Cooking Time: 24 minutes
Servings: 4

Ingredients:

- 4 medium potatoes, peeled and cleaned
- 1 medium onion, chopped
- 1 beaten egg
- ¼ cup milk
- 2 tablespoons unsalted butter
- ½ teaspoon garlic powder
- ¼ teaspoon salt
- 3 tablespoons all-purpose flour
- Pepper as needed

Directions:

1. Peel your potatoes and shred them up
2. Soak the shredded potatoes under cold water to remove starch
3. Drain the potatoes
4. Take a bowl and add eggs, milk, butter, garlic powder, salt, and pepper
5. Add in flour
6. Mix well
7. Add the shredded potatoes
8. Preheat Ninja Foodi by pressing the "AIR CRISP" option and setting it to "390 Degrees F" and timer to 24 minutes
9. let it preheat until you hear a beep
10. Add ¼ cup of the potato pancake batter to your cooking basket and cook for 12 minutes until the golden-brown texture is seen
11. Enjoy!

Nutritional Values (Per Serving):

- Calories: 240
- Fat: 11 g
- Saturated Fat: 4 g
- Carbohydrates: 33 g
- Fiber: 2 g
- Sodium: 259 mg
- Protein: 6

Early Morning Bacon Egg Muffins

Prep Time: 5 minutes
Cooking Time: 7-10 minutes
Servings: 4

Ingredients:

- 1 whole egg
- 2 streaky bacon
- 1 English muffin
- Salt and pepper to taste

Directions:

1. Pre-heat Ninja Foodi by pressing the "AIR CRISP" option and setting it to "200 Degrees F" and timer to 10 minutes
2. let it pre-heat until you hear a beep
3. Take an ovenproof bowl and crack in an egg
4. Take Ninja Foodi cooking basket and add bacon, egg, and muffin into Fryer
5. Cook for 7 mutes
6. Assemble muffin done by packing bacon and egg on top of English muffin
7. Serve and enjoy!

Nutritional Values (Per Serving):

- Calories: 600
- Fat: 40 g
- Saturated Fat: 10 g
- Carbohydrates: 30 g
- Fiber: 5 g
- Sodium: 526 mg
- Protein: 24 g

Magical Sausage and Kale

Prep Time: 10 minutes
Cooking Time: 10 minutes
Servings: 4

Ingredients:

- 1 medium sweet yellow onion
- 4 medium eggs
- 4 sausage links
- 2 cups kale, chopped
- 1 cup mushrooms
- Olive oil as needed

Directions:

1. Take your Ninja Foodi Grill and open lid, arrange grill grate and close top
2. Preheat Ninja Foodi by pressing the "GRILL" option and setting it to "HIGH" and timer to 5 minutes
3. let it preheat until you hear a beep
4. Arrange sausages over grill grate, lock lid and cook for 2 minutes, flip sausages and cook for 3 minutes more
5. Take sausages out
6. Take a baking pan and spread onion, kale, mushrooms, sausages and crack eggs on top
7. Arrange pan inside the grill and used the "BAKE" option to bake it at 350 degrees F for 5 minutes
8. Once done, open lid and serve
9. Enjoy!

Nutritional Values (Per Serving):

- Calories: 236
- Fat: 12 g
- Saturated Fat: 2 g
- Carbohydrates: 17 g
- Fiber: 4 g
- Sodium: 369 mg
- Protein: 18 g

Airy Mac and Cheese

Prep Time: 10 minutes
Cooking Time: 10 minutes
Servings: 4

Ingredients:

- 1 cup elbow macaroni
- ½ cup broccoli
- ½ cup warmed milk
- 1 and ½ cheddar cheese, grated
- Salt and pepper to taste
- 1 tablespoon parmesan cheese, grated

Directions:

1. Pre-heat Ninja Foodi by pressing the "AIR CRISP" option and setting it to "400 Degrees F" and timer to 10 minutes
2. let it pre-heat until you hear a beep
3. Take a pot and add water, allow it to boil
4. Add macaroni and veggies and broil for about 10 minutes until the mixture is Al Dente
5. Drain the pasta and vegetables
6. Toss the pasta and veggies with cheese
7. Season with some pepper and salt and transfer the mixture to your Foodi
8. Sprinkle some more parmesan on top and cook for about 15 minutes.
9. Allow it to cool for about 10 minutes once done
10. Enjoy!

Nutritional Values (Per Serving):

- Calories: 180
- Fat: 11 g
- Saturated Fat: 3 g
- Carbohydrates: 14 g
- Fiber: 2 g
- Sodium: 147 mg
- Protein: 6 g

Cool Potato Pancakes

Prep Time: 10 minutes
Cooking Time: 24 minutes
Servings: 4

Ingredients:

- 4 medium potatoes, peeled and cleaned
- 1 medium onion, chopped
- 1 beaten egg
- ¼ cup milk
- 2 tablespoons unsalted butter
- ½ teaspoon garlic powder
- ¼ teaspoon salt
- 3 tablespoons all-purpose flour
- Pepper as needed

Directions:

1. Peel your potatoes and shred them up
2. Soak the shredded potatoes under cold water to remove starch
3. Drain the potatoes
4. Take a bowl and add eggs, milk, butter, garlic powder, salt, and pepper
5. Add in flour
6. Mix well
7. Add the shredded potatoes
8. Pre-heat Ninja Foodi by pressing the "AIR CRISP" option and setting it to "390 Degrees F" and timer to 24 minutes
9. let it pre-heat until you hear a beep
10. Add ¼ cup of the potato pancake batter to your cooking basket and cook for 12 minutes until the golden-brown texture is seen
11. Enjoy!

Nutritional Values (Per Serving):

- Calories: 240
- Fat: 11 g
- Saturated Fat: 4 g
- Carbohydrates: 33 g
- Fiber: 2 g
- Sodium: 259 mg
- Protein: 6 g

Original French Pineapple Toast

Prep Time: 5-10 minutes
Cooking Time: 15 minutes
Servings: 4

Ingredients:

- 10 bread slices
- ¼ cup of sugar
- ¼ cup milk
- 3 large whole eggs
- 1 cup of coconut milk
- 10 slices pineapple, peeled
- ½ cup coconut flakes
- Cooking spray as needed

Directions:

1. Take a mixing bowl and whisk in coconut milk, sugar, eggs, milk and stir well
2. Dup breads in the mixture and keep the mon the side for 2 minutes
3. Pre-heat Ninja Foodi by pressing the "GRILL" option and setting it to "MED" and timer to 15 minutes
4. Let it pre-heat until you hear a beep
5. Arrange bread slices over grill grate, lock lid and cook for 2 minutes. Flip and cook for 2 minutes more, let them cook until the timer reads 0
6. Repeat with remaining slices, serve and enjoy!

Nutritional Values (Per Serving):

- Calories: 202
- Fat: 15 g
- Saturated Fat: 3 g
- Carbohydrates: 49 g
- Fiber: 3 g
- Sodium: 524 mg
- Protein: 8 g

Blister Green Beans

Prep Time: 5 minutes
Cooking Time: 10 minutes
Servings: 4

Ingredients:

- 1-pound green beans, trimmed
- 2 tablespoons vegetable oil
- 1 lemon, juiced
- Pinch of red pepper flakes
- Flaky sea salt as needed
- Fresh ground black pepper as needed

Directions:

1. Take a medium-sized bowl and add green beans
2. Preheat Ninja Foodi by pressing the "GRILL" option and setting it to "MAX" and timer to 10 minutes
3. Let it preheat until you hear a beep
4. Once preheated, transfer green beans to Grill Grate
5. Lock lid and let them grill for 8-10 minutes, making sure to toss them from time to time until all sides are blustered well
6. Squeeze lemon juice over green beans and top with red pepper flakes, season with salt and pepper

Nutritional Values (Per Serving):

- Calories: 100
- Fat: 7 g
- Saturated Fat: 1 g
- Carbohydrates: 10 g
- Fiber: 4 g
- Sodium: 30 mg
- Protein: 2 g

Tomato and Bacon Morning Omelet

Prep Time: 10 minutes
Cooking Time: 10 minutes
Servings: 4

Ingredients:

- 4 whole eggs, whisked
- 1 tablespoon cheddar, grated
- ¼ pound bacon, cooked and chopped
- 4 tomatoes, cubed
- 1 tablespoon parsley, chopped
- 1 tablespoon olive oil
- Salt and pepper to taste

Directions:

1. Take a small pan and place it over medium heat, add bacon and Sauté for 2 minutes until crisp
2. Take a bowl and add bacon, add remaining ingredients, and gently stir. Sprinkle cheese on top
3. Preheat Ninja Foodi by pressing the "BAKE" option and setting it to "400 Degrees F" and timer to 10 minutes
4. Let it preheat until you hear a beep
5. Pour mixture into a baking dish and transfer baking dish inside Ninja Foodi Grill, let it bake for 8 minutes
6. Serve and enjoy!

Nutritional Values (Per Serving):

- Calories: 311
- Fat: 16 g
- Saturated Fat: 4 g
- Carbohydrates: 23 g
- Fiber: 4 g
- Sodium: 149 mg
- Protein: 22 g

Chapter 2: Appetizers & Snacks Recipes

Fajita Skewers

Prep Time: 10 minutes
Cooking Time: 14 minutes
Servings: 8

Ingredients:

- 1-pound sirloin steak, cubed
- Olive oil, for drizzling
- 1 bunch scallions cut into large pieces
- 4 large bell pepper, cubed
- 1 pack tortillas, torn
- Salt to taste
- Black pepper, grounded

Directions:

1. Thread the steak, tortillas, scallions, and pepper on the skewers
2. Drizzle olive oil, salt, black pepper over the skewers
3. Pre-heat Ninja Foodi by pressing the "GRILL" option and setting it to "MED"
4. Once preheated, open the lid and place 4 skewers on the grill
5. Cover the lid and grill for 7 minutes
6. Keep rotating skewers for every 2 minutes
7. Serve warm and enjoy!

Nutritional Values (Per Serving):

- Calories: 353 kcal
- Carbs: 11 g
- Fat: 7.5 g.
- Protein: 13.1 g

Seared Tuna Salad

Prep Time: 10 minutes
Cooking Time: 6 minutes
Servings: 4

Ingredients:

- And 1/2-pounds ahi tuna, cut into four strips
- 2 tablespoons sesame oil
- 1(10 ounces) bag baby greens
- 2 tablespoons of rice wine vinegar
- 6 tablespoons extra-virgin olive oil
- 1/2 English cucumber, sliced
- 1/4 teaspoon of sea salt
- 1/2 teaspoon ground black pepper

Directions:

1. Supplement the flame broil mesh and close the hood
2. Pre-heat Ninja Foodi by pressing the "GRILL" option at and setting it to "MAX" and timer to 6 minutes
3. Take a small bowl, whisk together the rice vinegar, salt, and pepper
4. Slowly pour in the oil while whisking until vinaigrette is fully combined
5. Season the fish with salt and pepper, sprinkle with the sesame oil
6. Once it pre-heat until you hear a beep
7. Arrange the shrimp over the grill grate lock lid and cook for 6 minutes
8. Do not flip during cooking
9. Once cooked completely, top salad with tuna strip
10. Drizzle the vinaigrette over the top
11. Serve immediately and enjoy!

Nutritional Values (Per Serving):

- Calories: 427 kcal
- Carbs: 5 g
- Fat: 30 g.
- Protein: 36 g

Crispy Potato Cubes

Prep Time: 10 minutes
Cooking Time: 20 minutes
Servings: 4

Ingredients:

- 1-pound potato, peeled
- 1 tablespoon olive oil
- 1 teaspoon dried dill
- 1 teaspoon dried oregano
- 1/4 teaspoon chili flakes

Directions:

1. Pre-heat Ninja Foodi by squeezing the "AIR CRISP" alternative and setting it to "400 Degrees F" and timer to 20 minutes
2. Let it pre-heat until you hear a beep
3. Cut potatoes into cubes
4. Sprinkle potato cubes with dill, oregano and chili flakes
5. Transfer to Foodi Grill and cook for 15 minutes
6. Stir while cooking, once they are crunchy
7. Serve and enjoy!

Nutritional Values (Per Serving):

- Calories: 119 kcal
- Carbs: 20 g
- Fat: 4 g.
- Protein: 12 g

Crispy Rosemary Potatoes

Prep Time: 10 minutes
Cooking Time: 20 minutes
Servings: 4

Ingredients:

- 2 pounds baby red potatoes, quartered
- 2 tablespoons extra virgin olive oil
- 1/4 cup dried onion flakes
- 1/2 teaspoon onion powder
- 1/2 teaspoon garlic powder
- 1/4 teaspoon celery powder
- 1/4 teaspoon freshly ground black pepper
- 1/2 teaspoon dried parsley
- 1/2 teaspoon salt

Directions:

1. Take a large bowl and add all listed ingredients, toss well and coat them well
2. Pre-heat Ninja Foodi by squeezing the "AIR CRISP" alternative and setting it to "390 Degrees F" and clock to 20 minutes
3. Let it pre-heat until you hear a beep
4. Once preheated, add potatoes to the cooking basket
5. Lock and cook for 10 minutes, making sure to shake the basket and cook for 10 minutes more
6. Once done, check the crispiness, if it's alright, serve away.
7. If not, cook for 5 minutes more
8. Enjoy!

Nutritional Values (Per Serving):

- Calories: 232 kcal
- Carbs: 39 g
- Fat: 7 g.
- Protein: 4 g

Lemon-Garlic Shrimp Caesar Salad

Prep Time: 10 minutes
Cooking Time: 5 minutes
Servings: 4

Ingredients:

- 1-pound fresh jumbo shrimp
- 2 heads romaine lettuce, chopped
- 3/4 cup Caesar dressing
- 1/2 cup parmesan cheese, grated
- 1/2 lemon juice
- 3 garlic cloves, minced
- Sea salt
- Black pepper, grounded

Directions:

1. Addition the flame broils mesh and closes the hood. Pre-heat Ninja Foodi by pressing the "GRILL" option at and setting it to "MAX" and timer to 5 minutes
2. Take a large bowl; toss the shrimp with the lemon juice, garlic, salt, and pepper
3. Let it marinate while the grill is preheating
4. Once it pre-heat until you hear a beep
5. Arrange the shrimp over the grill grate lock lid and cook for 5 minutes
6. Toss the romaine lettuce with the Caesar dressing
7. Once cooked completely, remove the shrimp from the grill
8. Sprinkle with parmesan cheese
9. Serve and enjoy!

Nutritional Values (Per Serving):

- Calories: 279 kcal
- Carbs: 17 g
- Fat: 11 g.
- Protein: 30 g

Simple Crispy Brussels

Prep Time: 10 minutes
Cooking Time: 12 minutes
Servings: 4

Ingredients:

- 1-pound Brussels sprouts, halved
- 2 tablespoons olive oil, extra virgin
- 1/2 teaspoon ground black pepper
- 1 teaspoon salt
- 6 slices bacon, chopped

Directions:

1. Take a mixing bowl and add Brussels, olive oil, salt, pepper, and bacon
2. Pre-heat Ninja Foodi by squeezing the "AIR CRISP" alternative and setting it to "390 Degrees Fand clock to 12 minutes
3. Let it pre-heat until you hear a beep
4. Arrange Brussels over basket and lock lid, cook for 6 minutes, shake and cook for 6 minutes more
5. Serve and enjoy!

Nutritional Values (Per Serving):

- Calories: 279 kcal
- Carbs: 12 g
- Fat: 18 g.
- Protein: 14 g

Cajun Eggplant Appetizer

Prep Time: 5-10 minutes
Cooking Time: 10 minutes
Servings: 8

Ingredients:

- 2 small eggplants cut into slices
- 1/4 cup olive oil
- 2 tablespoons lime juice
- 3 teaspoons Cajun seasoning

Directions:

1. Coat the eggplant slices with oil, lemon juices and Cajun seasoning add the chicken wings and combine well to coat
2. Arrange the grill grate and close the lid
3. Pre-heat Ninja Foodi by pressing the "GRILL" option and setting it to "MED" and timer to 10 minutes
4. Let it pre-heat until you hear a beep
5. Arrange the eggplant slices over the grill grate, lock lid and cook for 5 minutes
6. Flip the chicken and close the lid, cook for 5 minutes more
7. Serve warm and enjoy!

Nutritional Values (Per Serving):

- Calories: 362 kcal
- Carbs: 16 g
- Fat: 11 g.
- Protein: 8 g

Portobello and Pesto Sliders

Prep Time: 10 minutes
Cooking Time: 8 minutes
Servings: 4

Ingredients:

- 8 small Portobello mushrooms, trimmed with gills removed
- 1 tomato, sliced
- 2 tablespoons canola oil
- 1/2 cup pesto
- 1/2 cup micro greens
- 2 tablespoons balsamic vinegar
- 8 slider buns

Directions:

1. Addition the flame broils mesh and closes the hood
2. Pre-heat Ninja Foodi by pressing the "GRILL" option at and setting it to "HIGH" and timer to 8 minutes
3. Brush the mushrooms with oil and balsamic vinegar
4. Once it pre-heat until you hear a beep
5. Arrange the mushrooms over the grill grate lock lid and cook for 8 minutes
6. Once cooked, removed the mushrooms from the grill and layer on the buns with tomato, pesto, and micro greens
7. Serve immediately and enjoy!

Nutritional Values (Per Serving):

- Calories: 373 kcal
- Carbs: 33 g
- Fat: 22 g.
- Protein: 12 g

Healthy Onion Rings

Prep Time: 10 minutes
Cooking Time: 10 minutes
Servings: 4

Ingredients:

- 1/4 teaspoon salt
- 1 egg
- 3/4 cup milk
- 1 tablespoon baking powder
- 3/4 cup breadcrumbs
- 1 large onion
- 1 cup flour
- 1 teaspoon paprika

Directions:

1. Pre-heat Ninja Foodi by squeezing the "AIR CRISP" alternative and setting it to "340 Degrees F" and timer to 10 minutes
2. Let it pre-heat until you hear a beep
3. Take a bowl and whisk the egg, milk, salt, flour, paprika together
4. Slice the onion and separate into rings
5. Grease your Ninja Foodi Grill with cooking spray
6. Then dip the onion rings into batter and coat with breadcrumbs
7. Arrange them in Ninja Foodi Grill Cooking Basket
8. Cook for 10 minutes
9. Serve and enjoy!

Nutritional Values (Per Serving):

- Calories: 450 kcal
- Carbs: 56 g
- Fat: 13 g.
- Protein: 30 g

Bacon Brussels Delight

Prep Time: 5-10 minutes
Cooking Time: 12 minutes
Servings: 4

Ingredients:

- 6 slices bacon, chopped
- 1-pound Brussels sprouts, halved
- 1/2 teaspoon black pepper
- 1 tablespoon of sea salt
- 2 tablespoons olive oil, extra-virgin

Directions:

1. Take a mixing bowl and toss the Brussels sprouts, olive oil, bacon, salt, and black pepper
2. Arrange the crisping basket inside the pot
3. Pre-heat Ninja Foodi by squeezing the "AIR CRISP" setting at 390 degrees F and timer to 12 minutes
4. Let it pre-heat until you hear a beep
5. Arrange the Brussels sprout mixture directly inside the basket
6. Close the top lid and cook for 6 minutes, then shake the basket
7. Close the top lid and cook for 6 minutes more
8. Serve warm and enjoy!

Nutritional Values (Per Serving):

- Calories: 279 kcal
- Carbs: 12.5 g
- Fat: 18.5 g.
- Protein: 14.5 g

Honey Mustard Chicken Tenders

Prep Time: 5 minutes
Cooking Time: 3 minutes
Servings: 4

Ingredients:

- 2 pounds chicken tenders
- 1/2 cup Dijon mustard
- 1/2 cup walnuts
- 2 tablespoons honey
- 2 tablespoons olive oil
- 1 teaspoon black pepper, ground

Directions:

1. Grab a bowl, using a whisk mix the mustard, olive oil, honey, and pepper into it
2. Add the chicken and toss to coat
3. Grind the walnut in your food processor
4. Supplement the flame broil mesh and close the hood
5. Pre-heat Ninja Foodi by pressing the "GRILL" option and setting it to "HIGH" for 4 minutes
6. Toss the chicken tenders in the ground walnuts to coat them lightly
7. Grill the chicken tender for 3 minutes
8. Serve hot and enjoy!

Nutritional Values (Per Serving):

- Calories: 444 kcal
- Carbs: 26 g
- Fat: 20 g.
- Protein: 6 g

Honey Asparagus

Prep Time: 10 minutes
Cooking Time: 15 minutes
Servings: 4

Ingredients:

- 2 pounds asparagus, trimmed
- 1/2 teaspoon pepper
- 1 teaspoon salt
- 1/4 cup honey
- 2 tablespoons olive oil
- 4 tablespoons tarragon, minced

Directions:

1. Take a bowl and add asparagus, oil, salt, honey, pepper, tarragon and toss well
2. Pre-heat Ninja Foodi by pressing the "GRILL" option and setting it to "MED" and timer to 8 minutes
3. Let it pre-heat until you hear a beep
4. Arrange asparagus over grill grate, lock lid and cook for 4 minutes, flip asparagus and cook for 4 minutes more
5. Serve and enjoy!

Nutritional Values (Per Serving):

- Calories: 240 kcal
- Carbs: 31 g
- Fat: 15 g.
- Protein: 7 g

Chapter 3: Chicken and Poultry Recipes

Mesmerizing Alfredo Apple Chicken

Prep Time: 5-10 minutes
Cooking Time: 20 minutes
Servings: 4

Ingredients:

- ½ cup alfredo sauce
- ¼ cup blue cheese, crumbled
- 4 slices provolone cheese
- 4 teaspoons chicken seasoning
- 4 chicken breast, halved
- 1 tablespoon lemon juice
- 1 large apple, wedged

Directions:

1. Take a medium-sized bowl and add chicken breasts, season them well
2. Take another bowl and add lemon juice, apple
3. Pre-heat your Ninja Foodi in "GRILL" mode on the "MED" settings, setting the timer to 20 minutes
4. Once you hear the beep, arrange the prepared chicken over the grill grate
5. Cook for 8 minutes, flip and cook for 8 minutes more, remove the chicken
6. Grill marinated apples in the same process, 2 minutes per side
7. Serve the prepared chicken dish with alfredo sauce, blue cheese, pepper, and apple
8. Have fun!

Nutritional Values (Per Serving):

- Calories: 247
- Fat: 19 g
- Saturated Fat: 6 g
- Carbohydrates: 29 g
- Fiber: 6 g
- Sodium: 853 mg
- Protein: 14 g

The Tarragon Chicken Meal

Prep Time: 10 minutes |Cooking Time: 5 minutes
Servings: 4

Ingredients:

For Chicken

- 1 and ½ pounds chicken tenders
- Salt as needed
- 3 tablespoons tarragon leaves, chopped
- 1 teaspoon lemon zest, grated
- 2 tablespoons fresh lemon juice
- 2 tablespoons extra virgin olive oil

For Sauce

- 2 tablespoons fresh lemon juice
- 2 tablespoons butter, salted
- ½ cup heavy whip cream

Directions:

1. Prepare your chicken by taking a baking dish and arranging the chicken over the dish in a single layer
2. Season generously with salt and pepper
3. Sprinkle chopped tarragon and lemon zest all around the tenders
4. Drizzle lemon juice and olive oil on top
5. Let them sit for 10 minutes
6. Drain them well
7. Insert Grill Grate in your Ninja Foodi Grill and set to HIGH temperature
8. Set timer to 4 minutes
9. Once you hear the beep, place chicken tenders in your grill grate
10. Let it cook for 3-4 minutes until cooked completely
11. Do in batches if needed
12. Transfer the cooked chicken tenders to a platter
13. For the sauce, take a small-sized saucepan
14. Add cream, butter and lemon juice and bring to a boil
15. Once thickened enough, pour the mix over chicken
16. Serve and enjoy!
17. Serve and enjoy once ready!

Nutritional Values (Per Serving):

Calories: 263 |Fat: 18 g|Saturated Fat: 4 g|Carbohydrates: 7 g|Fiber: 1 g| Sodium: 363 mg|Protein: 19 g

Daisy Fresh Maple Chicken

Prep Time: 10 minutes
Cooking Time: 15 minutes
Servings: 4

Ingredients:

- 2 teaspoons onion powder
- 2 teaspoons garlic powder
- 3 garlic cloves, minced
- 1/3 cup soy sauce
- 1 cup maple syrup
- ¼ cup teriyaki sauce
- 1 teaspoon black pepper
- 2 pounds chicken wings, bone-in

Directions:

1. Take a medium-sized bowl and add soy sauce, garlic, pepper, maple syrup, garlic powder, onion powder, teriyaki sauce and mix well
2. Add the chicken wings to the mixture and coat it gently
3. Preheat your Ninja Foodi Grill in MED mode, setting the timer to 10 minutes
4. Once you hear a beep, arrange your prepared wings in the grill grate
5. Cook for 5 minutes, flip and cook for 5 minutes more until the internal temperature reaches 165 degrees F
6. Serve!

Nutritional Values (Per Serving):

- Calories: 543
- Fat: 26 g
- Saturated Fat: 6 g
- Carbohydrates: 46 g
- Fiber: 4 g
- Sodium: 648 mg
- Protein: 42 g

BBQ Chicken Drumlets

Prep Time: 5-10 minutes
Cooking Time: 12 minutes
Servings: 5

Ingredients:

- 1/3 cup spice seasoning
- ½ tablespoon Worcestershire sauce
- 1 teaspoon dried onion, chopped
- 1 tablespoon bourbon
- 1 tablespoon brown sugar
- ½ cup ketchup
- 1 pinch salt
- 2 teaspoons seasoned BBQ
- 6 chicken drumlets

Directions:

1. Take a deep pan and add listed ingredients except for drumlets, stir the mixture well
2. Place it over medium heat, and stir cook for 8-10 minutes
3. Keep the mix on the side
4. Pre-heat your Ninja Foodi Grill to "MED" mode and set the timer to 12 minutes
5. Once you hear beep arrange the drumsticks over grill grate and brush half of your prepared sauce
6. Cook for 6 minutes, flip and brush more sauce, cook for 6 minutes more
7. Serve and enjoy once done with any remaining sauce
8. Enjoy!

Nutritional Values (Per Serving):

- Calories: 342
- Fat: 9 g
- Saturated Fat: 1 g
- Carbohydrates: 10 g
- Fiber: 2 g
- Sodium: 319 mg
- Protein: 12 g

Orange Grilled Chicken Meal

Prep Time: 5-10 minutes
Cooking Time: 15 minutes
Servings: 4

Ingredients:

- 12 chicken wings
- 2 tablespoons lime juice
- ¼ cup cilantro, chopped
- 2 teaspoons coriander, grounded
- 1 tablespoon canola oil
- 1/3 cup Sriracha chili sauce
- ¼ cup butter, melted
- 3 tablespoons honey
- ½ cup of orange juice
- ½ teaspoon garlic salt
- ¼ teaspoon ground black pepper

Directions:

1. Coat the chicken with oil, season with spices
2. Let it chill for 2 hours
3. Add listed ingredients and keep it on the side
4. Cook for 3-4 minutes in a saucepan
5. Pre-heat your Ninja Foodi by pressing the "GRILL" option and setting it to "MED."
6. Set your timer to 10 minutes
7. Let it pre-heat until it beeps
8. Arrange chicken over grill grate, cook for 5 minutes
9. Flip and let it cook for 5 minutes more
10. Serve with sauce on top
11. Serve and enjoy!

Nutritional Values (Per Serving):

- Calories: 320
- Fat: 14 g
- Saturated Fat: 4 g
- Carbohydrates: 19 g
- Fiber: 1 g
- Sodium: 258 mg
- Protein: 25 g

Grilled BBQ Turkey

Prep Time: 5-10 min.
Cooking Time: 30 min.
Servings: 5-6

Ingredients:

- 1/2 cup minced parsley
- 1/2 cup chopped green onions
- 4 garlic cloves, minced
- 1 cup Greek yogurt
- 1/2 cup lemon juice
- 1 teaspoon dried rosemary, crushed
- 1/3 cup canola oil
- 4 tablespoons minced dill
- 1 teaspoon salt
- 1/2 teaspoon pepper
- 1-3 pound turkey breast half, bone in

Directions:

1. In a mixing bowl, combine all the ingredients except the turkey. Add and coat the turkey evenly. Refrigerate for 8 hours to marinate.
2. Take Ninja Foodi Grill, arrange it over your kitchen platform, and open the top lid.
3. Arrange the grill grate and close the top lid.
4. Press "GRILL" and select the "HIGH" grill function. Adjust the timer to 30 minutes and then press "START/STOP." Ninja Foodi will start pre-heating.
5. Ninja Foodi is preheated and ready to cook when it starts to beep. After you hear a beep, open the top lid.
6. Arrange the turkey over the grill grate.
7. Close the top lid and cook for 15 minutes. Now open the top lid, flip the turkey.
8. Close the top lid and cook for 15 more minutes. Cook until the food thermometer reaches 350°F.
9. Slice and serve.

Nutritional Values (Per Serving):

- Calories: 426
- Fat: 8.5g
- Saturated Fat: 2g
- Trans Fat: 0g
- Carbohydrates: 22g
- Fiber: 3g
- Sodium: 594mg
- Protein: 38g

Classic BBQ Chicken Delight

Prep Time: 5-10 minutes
Cooking Time: 12 minutes
Servings: 4

Ingredients:

- 1/3 cup spice seasoning
- ½ tablespoon Worcestershire sauce
- 1 teaspoon dried onion, chopped
- 1 tablespoon bourbon
- 1 tablespoon brown sugar
- ½ cup ketchup
- 1 pinch salt
- 2 teaspoons BBQ seasoning
- 6 chicken drumsticks

Directions:

1. Take your saucepan and add listed ingredients except for drumsticks, stir cook for 8-10 minutes
2. Keep it on the side and let them cool
3. Pre-heat your Ninja Foodi Grill to MED and set the timer to 12 minutes
4. Once the beep sound is heard, arrange your drumsticks over the grill grate and brush with remaining sauce
5. Cook for 6 minutes, flip with some more sauce and grill for 6 minutes more
6. Enjoy once done!

Nutritional Values (Per Serving):

- Calories: 300
- Fat: 8 g
- Saturated Fat: 1 g
- Carbohydrates: 10 g
- Fiber: 1.5 g
- Sodium: 319 mg
- Protein: 12.5 g

Feisty Hot Pepper Wings Delight

Prep Time: 5-10 minutes
Cooking Time: 25 minutes
Servings: 4

Ingredients:

- ½ cup hot pepper sauce
- 2 tablespoons butter, melted
- 1 tablespoon coconut oil
- 1 pound chicken wings
- 1 tablespoon ranch salad dressing
- ½ teaspoon paprika

Directions:

1. Take a bowl and add chicken, oil, ranch dressing, and paprika. Transfer to your fridge and let it chill for about 30-60 minutes
2. Take another bowl and add the pepper sauce alongside butter
3. Pre-heat your Ninja Foodi Grill in MED mode, with a timer set to 25 minutes
4. Arrange the chicken wings over the grill grate
5. Cook for 25 minutes
6. Serve once done with the pepper sauce
7. Enjoy!

Nutritional Values (Per Serving):

- Calories: 510
- Fat: 24 g
- Saturated Fat: 7 g
- Carbohydrates: 6 g
- Fiber: 0.5 g
- Sodium: 841 mg
- Protein: 54 g

Juicy Moroccan Chicken Roast

Prep Time: 5-10 minutes
Cooking Time: 22 minutes
Servings: 4

Ingredients:

- ¼ teaspoon red pepper flakes, crushed
- 2 teaspoons paprika
- 2 teaspoons cumin, ground
- ½ teaspoon fresh flat-leaf parsley, chopped
- 1/3 cup olive oil
- ½ teaspoon salt
- 4 garlic cloves, chopped
- 4 skinless, boneless chicken thighs
- 3 tablespoons plain yogurt

Directions:

1. Add garlic, yogurt, salt, oil to your food processor and blend well
2. Take a mixing bowl and add red pepper flakes, chicken, paprika, cumin, parsley, garlic and mix
3. Let the chicken marinate for about 2-4 hours
4. Pre-heat your Ninja Foodi in "ROAST" mode, setting the temperature to "400 degrees F" and the time to 23 minutes
5. Once you hear the beep, arrange the chicken directly in the cooking pot
6. Let them cook for 15 minutes, flip and cook until the timer hits zero
7. Serve and enjoy once done!

Nutritional Values (Per Serving):

- Calories: 321
- Fat: 24 g
- Saturated Fat: 5 g
- Carbohydrates: 6 g
- Fiber: 2 g
- Sodium: 602 mg
- Protein: 21 g

Excellent Chicken Tomatino

Prep Time: 5-10 minutes
Cooking Time: 12 minutes
Servings: 4

Ingredients:

- ½ teaspoon salt
- 1 garlic clove, minced
- 2 tablespoons olive oil
- ¾ cup vinegar
- 8 plum tomatoes
- ¼ cup fresh basil leaves
- 4 chicken breast, boneless and skinless

Directions:

1. Take your fine food processor and add olive oil, vinegar, salt, garlic, and basil. Blend the mixture well until you have a smooth texture
2. Add tomatoes and blend once again
3. Take a mixing bowl and add tomato mix, chicken and mix well
4. Let the mixture chill for 1-2 hours
5. Pre-heat your Ninja Foodi Grill to HIGH and set the timer to 6 minutes
6. Once you hear the beep, arrange your prepared chicken over the grill grate
7. Cook for 3 minutes more
8. Flip the chicken and cook for 3 minutes more
9. Once properly cooked, serve and enjoy!

Nutritional Values (Per Serving):

- Calories: 400
- Fat: 5 g
- Saturated Fat: 3 g
- Carbohydrates: 18 g
- Fiber: 3 g
- Sodium: 230 mg
- Protein: 23 g

Glamorous Turkey Burger

Prep Time: 10 minutes
Cooking Time: 40 minutes
Servings: 4

Ingredients:

- 1 large red onion, chopped
- ½ teaspoon pepper
- ¼ teaspoon salt
- 1 cup feta cheese, crumbled
- 2/3 cup sun-dried tomatoes, chopped
- 6 burger buns, sliced in half
- 2 pounds lean turkey, grounded
- 3 ounces plain granola

Directions:

1. Take a medium-sized mixing bowl and add listed ingredients
2. Combine them well and make 6 patties out of the mixture
3. Pre-heat your Ninja Foodi Grill in MED mode setting the timer to 14 minutes
4. Wait till you hear the beep
5. Transfer the patties to your Ninja Foodi Grill Grate
6. Cook for 7 minutes
7. Serve by placing them in your burger buns
8. Enjoy!

Nutritional Values (Per Serving):

- Calories: 298
- Fat: 16 g
- Saturated Fat: 4 g
- Carbohydrates: 32 g
- Fiber: 4 g
- Sodium: 168 mg
- Protein: 27 g

Majestic Alfredo Chicken

Prep Time: 5-10 minutes
Cooking Time: 20 minutes
Servings: 4

Ingredients:

- ½ cup alfredo sauce
- ¼ cup blue cheese, crumbled
- 4 slices provolone cheese
- 4 teaspoons chicken seasoning
- 4 chicken breasts, halved
- 1 tablespoon lemon juice
- 1 large apple wedged

Directions:

1. Take a medium-sized bowl and add chicken, alongside the seasoning
2. Take another bowl and toss the apple with lemon juice
3. Pre-heat your Ninja Foodi Grill in MED mode, set timer to 16 minutes
4. Wait until you hear a beep sound
5. Arrange chicken pieces to the grill grate and cook for about 8 minutes, flip and cook for 8 minutes
6. Transfer the apple to the grill and cook for 4 minutes, giving 2 minutes to each side
7. Serve grilled chicken with the blue cheese, apple, alfredo sauce
8. Enjoy!

Nutritional Values (Per Serving):

- Calories: 247
- Fat: 19 g
- Saturated Fat: 3 g
- Carbohydrates: 29 g
- Fiber: 2 g
- Sodium: 850 mg
- Protein: 14 g

Awesome Baked Soy Chicken

Prep Time: 5-10 minutes
Cooking Time: 25 minutes
Servings: 5

Ingredients:

- 12 chicken thighs, skinless
- 1 tablespoon cornstarch
- ¼ cup apple cider vinegar
- 1 garlic clove, minced
- ½ cup of soy sauce
- 1 tablespoon cold water
- ½ cup white sugar
- ½ teaspoon ground ginger
- ¼ teaspoon ground pepper

Directions:

1. Add cornstarch water, white sugar, soy sauce, apple cider, vinegar, garlic, ginger, and pepper into a mixing bowl
2. Mix and combine them well
3. Season chicken with salt and pepper
4. Take your cooking pan and grease well with oil
5. Then add chicken and soy sauce mix on top
6. Pre-heat your Ninja Foodi by pressing the "BAKE" option and setting it to 350 degrees F
7. Set the timer to 25 minutes
8. Allow it to pre-heat until it beeps
9. Arrange the pan over grill grate and close the lid
10. Cook for 25 minutes
11. Serve and enjoy!

Nutritional Values (Per Serving):

- Calories: 570
- Fat: 19 g
- Saturated Fat: 5 g
- Carbohydrates: 23 g
- Fiber: 1 g
- Sodium: 600 mg
- Protein: 40 g

Feta Turkey Burgers

Prep Time: 10 min.
Cooking Time: 16 min.
Servings: 8

Ingredients:

- 2 1/2 cups spinach, chopped
- 3 garlic cloves, minced
- 1 tablespoon avocado oil
- 2 shallots, chopped
- 2/3 cup feta cheese, crumbled
- 1/2 teaspoon salt
- 1/4 teaspoon pepper
- 3/4 teaspoon Greek seasoning
- 2 pounds turkey ground
- 8 hamburger buns, split

Directions:

1. Stir-cook all the shallots for 2 minutes in a saucepan with some oil until softened. Add the spinach and garlic; cook until wilts.
2. In a mixing bowl, add the spinach mixture. Add the seasoning, beef, and feta cheese. Combine the ingredients to mix well with each other. Prepare 8 patties from the mixture.
3. Take Ninja Foodi Grill, arrange it over your kitchen platform, and open the top lid. Arrange the grill grate and close the top lid.
4. Press "GRILL" and select the "MED" grill function. Adjust the timer to 16 minutes and then press "START/STOP." Ninja Foodi will start pre-heating.
5. Ninja Foodi is preheated and ready to cook when it starts to beep. After you hear a beep, open the top lid.
6. Arrange two patties over the grill grate.
7. Close the top lid and cook for 8 minutes. Now open the top lid, flip the patties.
8. Close the top lid and cook for 8 more minutes — grill remaining patties in the same manner.
9. Prepare the burgers with your choice of toppings and buns; enjoy!

Nutritional Values (Per Serving):

- Calories: 328
- Fat: 12.5g
- Saturated Fat: 3g
- Trans Fat: 0g
- Carbohydrates: 31.5g
- Fiber: 6g
- Sodium: 464mg
- Protein: 39.5g

Chapter 4: Beef and Pork Recipes

All-Time Pineapple Steak

Prep Time: 5-10 minutes
Cooking Time: 8 minutes
Servings: 5

Ingredients:

- ½ medium pineapple, cored and diced
- 1 jalapeno pepper, seeded and stemmed, diced
- 1 medium red onion, diced
- 4 fillet mignon steak, (6-8 ounces)
- 1 tablespoon canola oil
- Salt and pepper to taste
- 1 tablespoon lime juice
- ¼ cup cilantro, chopped
- Chili powder and ground coriander

Directions:

1. Rub fillets with oil all over the steak and season with salt and pepper
2. Set you Ninja Foodi to GRILL mode and select HIGH, adjust the timer to 8 minutes
3. Let it preheat until you hear a beep
4. Arrange fillets over grill grate, cook for 4m minutes
5. Flip and cook for 4 minutes more until internal temperature reaches 125 degrees F
6. Take a bowl and add pineapple, onion, jalapeno
7. Add lime juice, cilantro, chili powder, coriander, and mix
8. Serve fillets with pineapple mix and serve
9. Enjoy!

Nutritional Values (Per Serving):

- Calories: 536
- Fat: 22 g
- Saturated Fat: 7 g
- Carbohydrates: 21 g
- Fiber: 4 g
- Sodium: 286 mg
- Protein: 58 g

Green Apple and Pork Roast

Prep Time: 10 minutes
Cooking Time: 23 minutes
Servings: 4

Ingredients:

- ¾ cup red wine
- 4 garlic cloves, minced
- 1 and ½ pounds pork tenderloin, cubed
- 2 green apples, cored and cut into wedges
- 2 tablespoons butter, melted
- Pepper and salt to taste

Directions:

1. Take your baking pan and grease with cooking spray, add ingredients and mix them
2. Pre-heat Ninja Foodi by pressing the "ROAST" option and setting it to "360 degrees F" and timer to 223minutes
3. Let it pre-heat until you hear a beep
4. Transfer baking dish to your Ninja Foodi Grill and let it bake until the timer runs out
5. Serve and enjoy once ready!

Nutritional Values (Per Serving):

- Calories: 426
- Fat: 17 g
- Saturated Fat: 4 g
- Carbohydrates: 15 g
- Fiber: 2 g
- Sodium: 256 mg
- Protein: 42 g

Lamb and Garlic Sauce

Prep Time: 10 minutes
Cooking Time: 5-10 minutes
Servings: 4

Ingredients:

- 1 garlic bulb
- 3 tablespoons olive oil
- 1 tablespoon fresh oregano, chopped
- Fresh ground black pepper
- 8 lamb chops

Directions:

1. Pre-heat Ninja Foodi by pressing the "AIR CRISP" option and setting it to "392 Degrees F" and timer to 10 minutes
2. Take a garlic bulb and coat with olive oil
3. Roast bulb for 12 minutes in Ninja Foodi Grill
4. Take a bowl and add salt, olive oil, and pepper
5. Coat lamb chops with a ½ tablespoon of herb/oil mix and lets it marinate for 5 minutes
6. Remove the bulb from coking tray and add lamb to the Grill, cook for 5 minutes
7. Squeeze garlic clove between your thumb and index finger over the herb oil mix, season with salt and pepper
8. Serve the lamb chops with garlic sauce
9. Enjoy!

Nutritional Values (Per Serving):

- Calories: 370
- Fat: 35 g
- Saturated Fat: 6 g
- Carbohydrates: 1 g
- Fiber: 0.3 g
- Sodium: 160 mg
- Protein: 15 g

Authentic Asian Apple Steak

Prep Time: 10 minutes
Cooking Time: 15-20 minutes
Servings: 4

Ingredients:

- 3 tablespoons sesame oil
- 3 tablespoons brown sugar
- 1 and ½ pounds beef tips
- 4 garlic cloves, minced
- ½ apple, peeled and grated
- 1/3 cup soy sauce
- 1 teaspoon ground black pepper
- Salt and pepper to taste

Directions:

1. Take your mixing bowl and add garlic, apple, sesame oil, sugar, soy sauce, pepper and salt
2. Add remaining ingredients and mix well
3. Add beef and coat for 1-2 hours, let it marinate
4. Pre-heat Ninja Foodi by pressing the GRILL" option and set it to "MED" and timer to 14 minutes
5. Let it pre-heat until you hear a beep
6. Arrange beef over grill grate, lock lid and cook for until timer reads 11 minutes
7. After that, cook until the internal temperature reaches 145 degrees F, cook for 3 minutes more if needed
8. Serve and enjoy!

Nutritional Values (Per Serving):

- Calories: 517
- Fat: 29 g
- Saturated Fat: 5 g
- Carbohydrates: 16 g
- Fiber: 4 g
- Sodium: 1198 mg
- Protein: 36 g

Original Korean Pork

Prep Time: 5-10 minutes
Cooking Time: 8 minutes
Servings: 4

Ingredients:

- 2 pounds pork, cut into 1/8-inch slices
- 5 garlic cloves, minced
- 3 tablespoons green onion, minced
- 1 yellow onion, sliced
- ½ cup of soy sauce
- ½ cup brown sugar
- 3 tablespoons Korean Red Chili Paste
- 2 tablespoons sesame seeds
- 3 teaspoons black pepper
- Red pepper flakes

Directions:

1. Take a zip bag and add listed ingredients, shake well and let it chill for 6-8 hours
2. Preheat Ninja Foodi by pressing the "GRILL" option and setting it to "MED" and timer to 8 minutes
3. Let it preheat until you hear a beep
4. Arrange sliced pork over grill grate, lock lid and cook for 4 minutes
5. Flip pork and cook for 4 minutes more, serve warm and enjoy with some chopped lettuce

Nutritional Values (Per Serving):

- Calories: 621
- Fat: 31 g
- Saturated Fat: 12 g
- Carbohydrates: 29 g
- Fiber: 3 g
- Sodium: 1428 mg
- Protein: 53 g

Green Pesto Ala Beef

Prep Time: 10 minutes
Cooking Time: 14 minutes
Servings: 4

Ingredients:

- 4 beef (6 ounces) tenderloin steak
- 10 ounces baby spinach, chopped
- 4 cups penne pasta, uncooked
- 4 cups grape tomatoes, halved
- ½ cup walnuts, chopped
- 2/3 cup pesto
- ½ cup feta cheese, crumbled
- ½ teaspoon salt
- ½ teaspoon pepper

Directions:

1. Prepare the pasta as per the given instructions on the pack
2. Drain and rinse, then keep this pasta aside
3. Season the tenderloin steaks with salt and pepper
4. Preheat Ninja Foodi by pressing the "GRILL" option and setting it to "HIGH" for 7 minutes
5. Once it preheats until you hear a beep, open the lid
6. Place the steaks in the grill grate and cook for 7 minutes
7. Flip it and cook for 7 minutes
8. Take a bowl and toss the pasta with spinach, tomatoes, walnuts, and pesto
9. Garnish with cheese
10. Serve and enjoy!

Nutritional Values (Per Serving):

- Calories: 361
- Fat: 5 g, Saturated Fat: 1 g
- Carbohydrates: 16 g
- Fiber: 4 g
- Sodium: 269 mg
- Protein: 33 g

Premium Salsa Avocado Steak

Prep Time: 5-10 minutes
Cooking Time: 18 minutes
Servings: 4

Ingredients:

- 1 cup cilantro leaves
- 2 ripe avocados, diced
- 2 cups salsa Verde
- 2 beef lank steak, diced
- ½ teaspoon salt
- ½ teaspoon pepper
- 2 medium tomatoes, seeded and diced

Directions:

1. Rub beef steak with salt and pepper, season well
2. Pre-heat Ninja Foodi by pressing the "GRILL" option and setting it to "MED" and timer to 18 minutes
3. Let it pre-heat until you hear a beep
4. Arrange diced steak over grill grate, lock lid and cook for 9 minutes
5. Flip and cook for 9 minutes more
6. Take a blender and blend in salsa, cilantro
7. Serve with grilled steak, with blended salsa, tomato, and avocado
8. Enjoy!

Nutritional Values (Per Serving):

- Calories: 520
- Fat: 31 g
- Saturated Fat: 9 g
- Carbohydrates: 38 g
- Fiber: 2 g
- Sodium: 301 mg
- Protein: 41 g

Beef with Pesto

Prep Time: 10 minutes
Cooking Time: 14 minutes
Serving: 4

Ingredients:

- 4 cups penne pasta, uncooked
- 10 oz. fresh baby spinach, chopped
- 4 beef (6 oz. tenderloin steaks
- 1/2 teaspoon salt
- 1/2 teaspoon pepper
- 4 cups grape tomatoes, halved
- 1/2 cup chopped walnuts
- 2/3 cup pesto
- 1/2 cup crumbled feta cheese

Directions:

1. At first, prepared the pasta as per the given instructions on the pack.
2. Drain and rinse, then keep this pasta aside.
3. Now season the tenderloin steaks with salt and pepper.
4. Prepare and preheat the Ninja Foodi Grill on a High-temperature setting.
5. Once it is preheated, open the lid and place the steaks on the grill.
6. Cover the Ninja Foodi Grill's lid and let it grill on the "Grilling Mode" for 7 minutes.
7. Flip the steaks and continue grilling for another 7 minutes
8. Toss the pasta with spinach, tomatoes, walnuts, and pesto in a bowl.
9. Slice the grilled steak and top the salad with the steak.
10. Garnish with cheese.
11. Enjoy.

Nutritional Values (Per Serving):

- Calories 361
- Total Fat 16 g
- Saturated Fat 5 g
- Cholesterol 114 mg
- Sodium 515 mg
- Total Carbs 19.3 g
- Fiber 0.1 g
- Sugar 18.2 g
- Protein 33.3 g

Traditional Avocado Grill Salad

Prep Time: 5-10 minutes
Cooking Time: 18 minutes
Servings: 4

Ingredients:

- 1 cup cilantro leaves
- 2 ripe avocados, diced
- 2 cups salsa Verde
- 2 beef lank steak, diced
- ½ teaspoon salt
- ½ teaspoon pepper
- 2 medium tomatoes, seeded and diced

Directions:

1. Rub beef steak with salt and pepper, season well
2. Preheat Ninja Foodi by pressing the "GRILL" option and setting it to "MED" and timer to 18 minutes
3. Let it preheat until you hear a beep
4. Arrange diced steak over grill grate, lock lid and cook for 9 minutes
5. Flip and cook for 9 minutes more
6. Take a blender and blend in salsa, cilantro
7. Serve with grilled steak, with blended salsa, tomato, and avocado
8. Enjoy!

Nutritional Values (Per Serving):

- Calories: 520
- Fat: 31 g
- Saturated Fat: 9 g
- Carbohydrates: 38 g
- Fiber: 2 g
- Sodium: 301 mg
- Protein: 41 g

Bourbon Flavored Pork Chops

Prep Time: 5-10 minutes
Cooking Time: 20 minutes
Servings: 5

Ingredients:

- 4 boneless pork chops
- Salt and pepper
- ¼ cup apple cider vinegar
- ¼ cup of soy sauce
- 3 tablespoons Worcestershire sauce
- 2 cups ketchup
- ¾ cup bourbon
- 1 cup packed brown sugar
- ½ tablespoon dry mustard powder

Directions:

1. Set you Ninja Foodi to GRILL mode and select MED, adjust the timer to 15 minutes
2. Let it preheat until you hear a beep
3. Arrange pork chops over grill grate, lock lid
4. Cook for 8 minutes, flip and cook for 2 minutes more If needed
5. Take a saucepan and heat remaining ingredients until the sauce boils
6. Lower heat to low and simmer for 20 minutes
7. Serve pork chops with the sauce
8. Enjoy!

Nutritional Values (Per Serving):

- Calories: 346
- Fat: 13 g
- Saturated Fat: 4 g
- Carbohydrates: 27 g
- Fiber: 0.4 g
- Sodium: 1324 mg
- Protein: 27 g

Beef Burgers

Prep Time: 15 minutes|Cooking Time: 18 minutes
Servings: 4

Ingredients:

For Burgers:
- 1-pound ground beef
- ½ cup panko breadcrumbs
- ¼ cup onion, chopped finely
- 3 tablespoons Dijon mustard

For Topping:
- 2 tablespoons Dijon mustard
- 1 tablespoon brown sugar

- 3 teaspoons low-sodium soy sauce
- 2 teaspoons fresh rosemary, chopped finely
- Salt, to taste

- 1 teaspoon soy sauce
- 4 Gruyere cheese slices

Directions:

1. In a large bowl, add all the ingredients and mix until well combined.
2. Make 4 equal-sized patties from the mixture.
3. Arrange the patties onto a cooking tray.
4. Arrange the drip pan at the bottom of the Ninja Foodi Grill cooking chamber.
5. Select "AIR CRISP" and then adjust the temperature to 370 degrees F.
6. Set the timer for 15 minutes and press the "Start."
7. When the display shows "Add Food" insert the cooking rack in the center position.
8. When the display shows "Turn Food," turn the burgers.
9. Meanwhile, for the sauce: In a small bowl, add the mustard, brown sugar, and soy sauce and mix well.
10. When cooking time is complete, remove the tray from Ninja Foodi and coat the burgers with the sauce.
11. Top each burger with 1 cheese slice.
12. Return the tray to the cooking chamber and select "Broil."
13. Set the timer for 3 minutes and press the "Start."
14. When cooking time is complete, remove the tray from Ninja Foodi and serve hot.

Nutritional Values (Per Serving):

Calories 402|Total Fat 18 g|Total Carbs 6.3 g|Fiber 0.8 g|Sugar 3 g|Protein 44.4 g

Fine Onion Roasted Beef

Prep Time: 5-10 minutes
Cooking Time: 30 minutes
Servings: 6

Ingredients:

- 2 sticks celery, sliced
- 1 bulb garlic, peeled and crushed
- Bunch of herbs
- 2 pounds topside beef
- 2 medium onion, chopped
- Salt and pepper to taste
- 1 tablespoon butter
- 3 tablespoons olive oil

Directions:

1. Take a mixing bowl and add listed ingredients, combine well with each other
2. Pre-heat Ninja Foodi by pressing the "ROAST" option and setting it to "380 Degrees F" and timer to 30 minutes
3. Let it pre-heat until you hear a beep
4. Arrange bowl mixture in your Nina Foodi Pan, cook until the timer reads zero
5. Serve and enjoy!

Nutritional Values (Per Serving):

- Calories: 320
- Fat: 17 g
- Saturated Fat: 3 g
- Carbohydrates: 11 g
- Fiber: 2 g
- Sodium: 632 mg
- Protein: 31 g

Chimichurri Sauce Steak

Prep Time: 10 minutes
Cooking Time: 10 minutes
Servings: 4

Ingredients:

- 16 ounces skirt steak
- Chimichurri Sauce
- 1 cup parsley, chopped
- ¼ cup mint, chopped
- 2 tablespoons oregano, chopped
- 3 garlic cloves, chopped
- 1 teaspoon crushed red pepper
- 1 tablespoon cumin, grounded
- 1 teaspoon cayenne pepper
- 2 teaspoons smoked paprika
- 1 teaspoon salt
- ¼ teaspoon pepper
- ¾ cup olive oil
- 3 tablespoons red wine vinegar

Directions:

1. Take a bowl and mix all of the ingredients listed under Chimichurri section and mix them well
2. Cut the steak into 2 pieces of 8-ounce portions
3. Take a resealable bag and add ¼ cup of Chimichurri alongside the steak pieces and shake them to ensure that steak is coated well
4. Allow it to chill in your fridge for 2-24 hours
5. Remove the steak from the fridge 30 minutes before cooking
6. Pre-heat Ninja Foodi by pressing the "AIR CRISP" option and setting it to "390 Degrees F" and timer to 10 minutes
7. Transfer the steak to your Ninja Foodi Grill and cook for about 8-10 minutes if you are looking for a medium-rare finish
8. Garnish with 2 tablespoons of Chimichurri sauce and enjoy!

Nutritional Values (Per Serving):

- Calories: 300
- Fat: 18 g
- Saturated Fat: 4 g
- Carbohydrates: 80 g
- Fiber: 4 g
- Sodium: 415 mg
- Protein: 13 g

Ranch Flavored Cauliflower Steak

Prep Time: 10 minutes

Cooking Time: 15 minutes

Servings: 4

Ingredients:

- 1 head cauliflower, stemmed and leaves removed
- ¼ cup canola oil
- ½ teaspoon garlic powder
- ½ teaspoon paprika
- Salt and pepper to taste
- 1 cup cheddar cheese, shredded
- Ranch dressing, garnish
- 4 slices bacon, cooked and crumbled
- 2 tablespoons chopped fresh chives

Directions:

1. Cut cauliflower from top to bottom into 2-inch steaks, reserve the remaining cauliflower to cook
2. Take a small-sized bowl and whisk in oil, garlic powder, paprika, season with salt and pepper
3. Brush each steak with oil mixture on both sides
4. Pre-heat Ninja Foodi by pressing the "GRILL" option and setting it to "MAX" and timer to 15 minutes
5. let it pre-heat until you hear a beep
6. Transfer steaks to Grill Grate, lock lid and grill for 10 minutes
7. After 10 minutes, flip steaks and top with ½ cup cheese
8. Lock lid and cook for 5 minutes more
9. Once done, drizzle with ranch dressing, top with bacon and chives
10. Enjoy!

Nutritional Values (Per Serving) :

- Calories: 720
- Fat: 19 g
- Saturated Fat: 19 g
- Carbohydrates: 11 g
- Fiber: 4 g
- Sodium: 1555 mg
- Protein: 32 g

Chapter 5: Fish and Seafood Recipes

Swordfish with Caper Sauce

Prep Time: 10 minutes
Cooking Time: 8 minutes
Servings: 4

Ingredients:

- Pepper as needed
- Salt as needed
- 2 tablespoon capers drained
- 1 tablespoon extra virgin olive oil
- 1 tablespoon lemon juice
- 1 lemon, sliced into 8 slices
- 4 tablespoons unsalted butter
- 4 swordfish steaks, 1 inch thick

Directions:

1. Take a large shallow bowl and whisk together the lemon juice and oil
2. Season with swordfish steaks with salt and pepper on each side, place in the oil mixture
3. Turn to coat both sides and refrigerate for 15 minutes
4. Insert the grill grate and close the hood
5. Pre-heat Ninja Foodi by pressing the "GRILL" option at and setting it to "MAX" and timer to 8 minutes
6. Let it pre-heat until you hear a beep
7. Arrange the swordfish over the grill grate, lock lid and cook for 9 minutes
8. Place a medium saucepan over medium heat and melt butter
9. Add the lemon slices and capers to the pan and cook for 1 minute
10. Then turn off the heat
11. Remove the swordfish from the grill and serve with caper sauce over it
12. Enjoy!

Nutritional Values (Per Serving):

- Calories: 472
- Fat: 31 g
- Saturated Fat: 6 g
- Carbohydrates: 2 g
- Fiber: 0.5 g
- Sodium: 540 mg
- Protein: 48 g

Caper Sauce and Swordfish

Prep Time: 10 minutes + marinate time
Cooking Time: 8 minutes
Servings: 4

Ingredients:

- Salt and pepper to taste
- 2 tablespoons caper, drained
- 1 tablespoon extra-virgin olive oil
- 1 tablespoon lemon juice
- 1 lemon, sliced into 8 slices
- 4 tablespoons butter, unsalted
- 4 swordfish steak, 1 inch thick

Directions:

1. Take a large bowl and add lemon juice and oil, whisk well
2. Season your steaks with salt and pepper on both sides, transfer the seasoned steaks to your oil mixture
3. Turn over and coat them generously, let them sit in your fridge for 15 minutes
4. Set your Ninja Foodi Grill to "MAX" with the timer set to 8 minutes
5. Once you hear the beep, arrange swordfish over grill grate and lock the lid
6. Cook until the timer runs out
7. Take a medium-sized saucepan and place it over medium heat, add butter and let it melt
8. Add lemon slices, capers to the pan and cook for 1 minute
9. Remove heat
10. Remove the swordfish from your grill and serve by pouring the prepared sauce over the steak
11. Serve and enjoy!

Nutritional Values (Per Serving):

- Calories: 472
- Fat: 31 g
- Saturated Fat: 6 g
- Carbohydrates: 2 g
- Fiber: 0.5 g
- Sodium: 540 mg
- Protein: 48 g

Excellent Garlic Salmon

Prep Time: 5-10 minutes
Cooking Time: 12 minutes
Servings: 3

Ingredients:

- 2 salmon fillets, 6 ounces each
- ¼ teaspoon fresh rosemary, minced
- 1 garlic clove, minced
- 1 teaspoon lemon zest, grated
- ¼ teaspoon salt
- ¼ teaspoon pepper

Directions:

1. Add all ingredients except salmon into your mixing bowl and mix well
2. Add salmon and combine them
3. Let it sit for 15 minutes
4. Pre-heat Ninja Foodi by pressing the "GRILL" option and setting it to "MED."
5. Cook for 6 minutes
6. Let it pre-heat until it beeps
7. Place salmon over the grill grate
8. Close the lid and cook for 3 minutes
9. Then flip and cook for 3 minutes more
10. Serve and enjoy!

Nutritional Values (Per Serving):

- Calories: 250
- Fat: 8 g
- Saturated Fat: 3g
- Carbohydrates: 22 g
- Fiber: 3 g
- Sodium: 370 mg
- Protein: 36 g

Salmon and Dill Sauce Meal

Prep Time: 10 minutes

Cooking Time: 20-25 minutes

Servings: 4

Ingredients:

- 4 salmon, each of 6 ounces
- 2 teaspoons olive oil
- 1 pinch salt

Dill Sauce

- ½ cup non-fat Greek Yogurt
- ½ cup sour cream
- Pinch of salt
- 2 tablespoons dill, chopped

Directions:

1. Pre-heat Ninja Foodi by pressing the "AIR CRISP" option and setting it to "270 Degrees F" and timer to 25 minutes
2. Wait until the appliance beeps
3. Drizzle cut pieces of salmon with 1 teaspoon olive oil
4. Season with salt
5. Take the cooking basket out and transfer salmon to basket, cook for 20-23 minutes
6. Take a bowl and add sour cream, salt, chopped dill, yogurt and mix well to prepare the dill sauce
7. Serve cooked salmon by pouring the sauce all over
8. Garnish with chopped dill and enjoy!

Nutritional Values (Per Serving):

- Calories: 600
- Fat: 45 g
- Saturated Fat: 6 g
- Carbohydrates: 5 g
- Fiber: 2 g
- Sodium: 422 mg
- Protein: 60 g

Spiced Up Grilled Shrimp

Prep Time: 5-10 minutes
Cooking Time: 6 minutes
Servings: 4

Ingredients:

- 2 tablespoons brown sugar
- 1 pound jumbo shrimp, peeled and deveined
- 2 tablespoons olive oil
- 1 tablespoon garlic powder
- 1 tablespoon paprika
- ½ teaspoon black pepper
- 1 teaspoon garlic salt

Directions:

1. Take a bowl and add listed ingredients gently mix
2. Let the mixture chill for 30-60 minutes
3. Preheat your Grill in MED mode setting timer to 6 minutes
4. Once you hear the beep, arrange your prepared shrimp over the grill grate
5. Lock and let it cook for 3 minutes
6. Flip and cook for 3 minutes more
7. Once done, serve and enjoy!

Nutritional Values (Per Serving):

- Calories: 370
- Fat: 27 g
- Saturated Fat: 3 g
- Carbohydrates: 23 g
- Fiber: 8 g
- Sodium: 182 mg
- Protein: 6 g

Mustard-y Crisped Up Cod

Prep Time: 5-10 minutes

Cooking Time: 10 minutes

Servings: 3

Ingredients:

- 1 large whole egg
- 1 teaspoon Dijon mustard
- ½ cup bread crumbs
- 1-pound cod filets
- ¼ cup all-purpose flour
- 1 tablespoon dried parsley
- 1 teaspoon paprika
- ½ teaspoon pepper

Directions:

1. Take fish fillets and slice them into 1 inch wide strips
2. Take a mixing bowl and whisk in eggs, add mustard and combine well
3. Add flour in another bowl
4. Take another bowl and add bread crumbs, dried parsley, paprika, black pepper and combine well
5. Coat strips with flour, then coat with egg mix, coat with crumbs at last
6. Preheat Ninja Foodi by pressing the "AIR CRISP" option and setting it to "390 Degrees F" and timer to 10 minutes
7. Let it preheat until you hear a beep
8. Arrange strips directly inside basket, lock lid and cook until the timer runs out
9. Serve and enjoy!

Nutritional Values (Per Serving):

- Calories: 200
- Fat: 4 g
- Saturated Fat: 1 g
- Carbohydrates: 17 g
- Fiber: 1 g
- Sodium: 214 mg
- Protein: 24 g

Succulent Baked Haddock

Prep Time: 5-10 minutes
Cooking Time: 13 minutes
Servings: 3

Ingredients:

- 1-pound haddock fillets
- ¼ cup parmesan cheese, grated
- ¼ cup butter, melted
- ¾ cup milk
- ¾ cup breadcrumbs
- ¼ teaspoon dried thyme, ground
- ¼ teaspoon salt

Directions:

1. Coat fish fillets in milk, season with salt
2. Set it aside
3. Add breadcrumbs, parmesan, cheese, thyme into a mixing bowl
4. Combine them well
5. Coat fillets in bread crumb mixture
6. Pre-heat Ninja your Foodi by pressing the "BAKE" option and setting it to 325 Degrees F
7. Set the timer to 13 minutes
8. Allow it to pre-heat until it beeps
9. Arrange fish fillets directly over Grill Grate and close the lid
10. Cook for 8 minutes
11. Then flip and cook for 5 minutes
12. Serve and enjoy!

Nutritional Values (Per Serving):

- Calories: 450
- Fat: 27 g
- Saturated Fat: 12 g
- Carbohydrates: 16 g
- Fiber: 22 g
- Sodium: 1056 mg
- Protein: 44 g

Spicy Cajun Shrimp

Prep Time: 10 minutes

Cooking Time: 7 minutes

Servings: 4

Ingredients:

- 1 and ¼ pound tiger shrimp, about 16-20 pieces
- ¼ teaspoon cayenne pepper
- ½ teaspoon old bay seasoning
- ¼ teaspoon smoked paprika
- 1 pinch of salt
- 1 tablespoon olive oil

Directions:

1. Pre-heat Ninja Foodi by pressing the "AIR CRISP" option and setting it to "390 Degrees F" and timer to 10 minutes
2. Take a mixing bowl and add ingredients (except shrimp), mix well
3. Dip the shrimp into spice mixture and oil
4. Transfer the prepared shrimp to your Ninja Foodi Grill cooking basket and cook for 5 minutes
5. Serve and enjoy!

Nutritional Values (Per Serving):

- Calories: 170
- Fat: 2 g
- Saturated Fat: 0.5 g
- Carbohydrates: 5 g
- Fiber: 2 g
- Sodium: 1236 mg
- Protein: 23 g

Homely BBQ Shrimp

Prep Time: 5-10 minutes
Cooking Time: 7 minutes
Servings: 2

Ingredients:

- ½ pound shrimps, large
- ½ orange, juiced
- 3 tablespoons chipotle in adobo sauce, minced
- ¼ cup BBQ sauce
- ¼ teaspoon salt

Directions:

1. Add all ingredients into a mixing bowl
2. Mix them well and keep it on the side
3. Pre-heat Ninja Foodi by pressing the "ROAST" option and set for 400 Degrees F
4. Then set the timer to 7 minutes
5. Let it pre-heat until it makes a beep
6. Arrange shrimps over Grill Grate and lock lid
7. Cook for 7 minutes
8. Serve and enjoy!

Nutritional Values (Per Serving):

- Calories: 173
- Fat: 2 g
- Saturated Fat: 0.5 g
- Carbohydrates: 21 g
- Fiber: 2 g
- Sodium: 1143 mg
- Protein: 17 g

Swordfish with Caper Sauce

Prep Time: 10 minutes
Cooking Time: 8 minutes
Servings: 4

Ingredients:

- Pepper as needed
- Salt as needed
- 2 tablespoon capers drained
- 1 tablespoon extra virgin olive oil
- 1 tablespoon lemon juice
- 1 lemon, sliced into 8 slices
- 4 tablespoons unsalted butter
- 4 swordfish steaks, 1 inch thick

Directions:

1. Take a large shallow bowl and whisk together the lemon juice and oil
2. Season with swordfish steaks with salt and pepper on each side, place in the oil mixture
3. Turn to coat both sides and refrigerate for 15 minutes
4. Insert the grill grate and close the hood
5. Pre-heat Ninja Foodi by pressing the "GRILL" option at and setting it to "MAX" and timer to 8 minutes
6. Let it pre-heat until you hear a beep
7. Arrange the swordfish over the grill grate, lock lid and cook for 9 minutes
8. Place a medium saucepan over medium heat and melt butter
9. Add the lemon slices and capers to the pan and cook for 1 minute
10. Then turn off the heat
11. Remove the swordfish from the grill and serve with caper sauce over it
12. Enjoy!

Nutritional Values (Per Serving):

- Calories: 472
- Fat: 31 g
- Saturated Fat: 6 g
- Carbohydrates: 2 g
- Fiber: 0.5 g
- Sodium: 540 mg
- Protein: 48 g

Awesome Shrimp Roast

Prep Time: 5-10 minutes

Cooking Time: 7 minutes

Servings: 2

Ingredients:

- 3 tablespoons chipotle in adobo sauce, minced
- ¼ teaspoon salt
- ¼ cup BBQ sauce
- ½ orange, juiced
- ½ pound large shrimps

Directions:

1. Take a mixing bowl and add all ingredients, mix well
2. Keep it on the side
3. Preheat Ninja Foodi by pressing the "ROAST" option and setting it to "400 Degrees F" and timer to 7 minutes
4. Let it preheat until you hear a beep
5. Arrange shrimps over Grill Grate and lock lid, cook until the timer runs out
6. Serve and enjoy!

Nutritional Values (Per Serving):

- Calories: 173
- Fat: 2 g
- Saturated Fat: 0.5 g
- Carbohydrates: 21 g
- Fiber: 2 g
- Sodium: 1143 mg
- Protein: 17 g

Home Haddock

Prep Time: 5-10 minutes
Cooking Time: 13 minutes
Servings: 3

Ingredients:

- ¼ teaspoon salt
- ¾ cup breadcrumbs
- ¼ cup parmesan cheese, grated
- ¼ teaspoon ground thyme
- ¼ cup butter, melted
- 1 pound haddock fillets
- ¾ cup milk

Directions:

1. Take the fish fillets and carefully dredge them in milk
2. Season them well with salt, keep them on the side
3. Take a medium-sized bowl, add cheese, thyme, parmesan, breadcrumbs, and mix
4. Take your fillets and coat them with breadcrumbs
5. Pre-heat your Ninja Foodi Grill in Bake mode to a temperature of 325 degrees F, setting the timer to 13 minutes
6. Once you hear the beep, the appliance is ready
7. Transfer the prepared fillets to Grill Grate and cook for 8 minutes, flip and cook for 5 minutes more
8. Once you have a flaky texture, serve, and enjoy!

Nutritional Values (Per Serving):

- Calories: 450
- Fat: 27 g
- Saturated Fat: 12 g
- Carbohydrates: 16 g
- Fiber: 22 g
- Sodium: 1056 mg
- Protein: 44 g

Crispy Crabby Patties

Prep Time: 5-10 minutes
Cooking Time: 10 minutes
Servings: 4

Ingredients:

- 12 ounces lump crabmeat
- 1 shallot, minced
- 2 tablespoons almond flour
- 2 tablespoons Dijon mustard
- 1 lemon, zest
- ¼ cup mayonnaise, low carb
- ¼ cup parsley, minced
- 1 egg, beaten
- Pepper and salt as needed

Directions:

1. Add all ingredients into a mixing bowl
2. Mix them well and prepare 4 meat from the mixture
3. Pre-heat Ninja Foodi by pressing the "AIR CRISP" option and setting it to 375 Degrees F
4. Set your timer to 10 minutes
5. Let it pre-heat until it beeps
6. Transfer patties to cooking basket and let them cook for 5 minutes
7. Flip and cook for 5 minutes more
8. Serve and enjoy once done!

Nutritional Values (Per Serving):

- Calories: 177
- Fat: 13 g
- Saturated Fat: 2 g
- Carbohydrates: 2.5 g
- Fiber: 0 g
- Sodium: 358 mg
- Protein: 11 g

Parmesan Fish Sticks with Malt Vinegar Dipping Sauce

Prep Time: 15 Minutes |Cook Time: 15 Minutes |Total Time: 30 Minutes
Servings: 4

Ingredients:

For Fish Sticks

- 1 pinch of salt and ground black pepper to taste
- ½ cup of panko bread crumbs
- ½ teaspoon of dried basil
- ½ cup of all-purpose flour
- 2 large eggs
- ¼ cup of grated parmesan cheese
- ½ teaspoon of dried oregano
- 1 tablespoon of olive oil or as needed
- 4 (6 ounces) halibut fillets, to be cut into 3x1/2-inch strips

Dipping Sauce

- 1/4 cup of mayonnaise
- ¼ cup of ketchup
- 1 ½ tablespoons of malt vinegar

Directions:

1. Preheat your Grill to 450OF (230OC). Then line your baking sheet with an aluminum foil.

2. Whisk flour, pepper, and salt together in a shallow bowl. Beat the eggs in another bowl until it turns frothy in about 30 seconds. Combine parmesan cheese, panko bread crumbs, oregano, and basil in another shallow bowl (that should be the third bowl you are using).

3. Next is to dredge the fish through the flour mixture until it becomes thoroughly coated. Shake off excess flour. Then dip the fish into the egg and allow excess egg to drip inside the bowl. Press the fish inside the panko mixture until it is completely coated. Arrange the coated fish on the prepared baking sheet. Then drizzle the olive oil over the fish.

4. Then cook in the already preheated Grill until the fish sticks become golden brown and flake easily when touched with a fork in about 15 minutes.

5. Mix ketchup, malt vinegar, and mayonnaise in a bowl and serve together with fish sticks.

Nutritional Values (Per Serving):

478 calories| Carbohydrates 26.7 grams 9% DV| Protein 43.5 grams 87% DV| Fat 22.7 grams 35% DV| Cholesterol 156.3 mg 52%| Sodium 554 mg 22% DV.

Daring Spicy Grilled Shrimp

Prep Time: 5-10 minutes

Cooking Time: 6 minutes

Servings: 4

Ingredients:

- 1 teaspoon garlic salt
- ½ teaspoon black pepper
- 1 tablespoon paprika
- 1 tablespoon garlic powder
- 2 tablespoons olive oil
- 1-pound jumbo shrimps, peeled and deveined
- 2 tablespoons brown sugar

Directions:

1. Take a mixing bowl and add listed ingredients to mix well
2. Let it chill and marinate for 30-60 minutes
3. Preheat Ninja Foodi by pressing the "GRILL" option and setting it to "MED" and timer to 6 minutes
4. Let it preheat until you hear a beep
5. Arrange prepared shrimps over grill grate, lock lid and cook for 3 minutes, flip and cook for 3 minutes more
6. Serve and enjoy!

Nutritional Values (Per Serving):

- Calories: 370
- Fat: 27 g
- Saturated Fat: 3 g
- Carbohydrates: 23 g
- Fiber: 8 g
- Sodium: 182 mg
- Protein: 6 g

Chapter 6: Vegetarian Recipes

Zucchini Parmesan Chips

Prep Time: 10 minutes
Cooking Time: 8 minutes
Serving: 10

Ingredients:

- ½ tsp. paprika
- ½ C. grated parmesan cheese
- ½ C. Italian breadcrumbs
- 1 lightly beaten egg
- 2 thinly sliced zucchinis

Directions:

1. Use a very sharp knife or mandolin slicer to slice zucchini as thinly as you can—Pat off extra moisture.
2. Beat egg with a pinch of pepper and salt and a bit of water.
3. Combine paprika, cheese, and breadcrumbs in a bowl.
4. Dip slices of zucchini into the egg mixture and then into breadcrumb mixture. Press gently to coat.
5. Insert the Crisper Basket, and close the hood. Select AIR CRISP, set the temperature to 350°F, and set the time to 8 minutes. Select START/STOP to begin preheating.
6. Air Frying.
7. With olive oil cooking spray, mist coated zucchini slices. Place into your air fryer in a single layer. Set temperature to 350°F, and set time to 8 minutes.
8. Sprinkle with salt and serve with salsa.

Nutritional Values (Per Serving):

- Calories 211
- Fat: 16 g
- Protein 8 g
- Sugar 10 g

Spicy Cajun Eggplant Meal

Prep Time: 5-10 minutes
Cooking Time: 10 minutes
Servings: 4

Ingredients:

- 2 tablespoons lime juice
- 3 teaspoons Cajun seasoning
- 2 small eggplant, cut into slices
- ¼ cup olive oil

Directions:

1. Coat eggplant slices with oil, lemon juice, Cajun seasoning
2. Pre-heat Ninja Foodi by pressing the "GRILL" option and setting it to "MED" and timer to 10 minutes
3. Let it pre-heat until you hear a beep
4. Arrange eggplant slices over the grill, lock the lid, and grill for 5 minutes. Flip and cook for 5 minutes more
5. Serve and enjoy!

Nutritional Values (Per Serving):

- Calories: 362
- Fat: 11 g
- Saturated Fat: 3 g
- Carbohydrates: 16 g
- Fiber: 2 g
- Sodium: 524 mg
- Protein: 8 g

Honey and Lime Salad

Prep Time: 5-10 minutes

Cooking Time: 4 minutes

Servings: 4

Ingredients:

- ½ pound strawberries washed, hulled and halved
- 1 can (9 ounces) pineapple chunks, drained
- 1 tablespoon lime juice, squeezed
- 6 tablespoons honey, divided
- 2 peaches, pitted and sliced

Directions:

1. Take a bowl and add pineapple, strawberries, peach, and 3 tablespoons, honey
2. Toss well
3. Pre-heat your Ninja Foodi Grill to MAX mode and set the timer to 4 minutes
4. Once you heart beeping sound, transfer fruits to the grill grate
5. Cook for 4 minutes
6. Take a small bowl and add remaining honey, lime juice, 1 tablespoon reserved pineapple juice
7. Once the fruits are cooked, transfer fruits to this mixture
8. Toss and serve
9. Enjoy!

Nutritional Values (Per Serving):

- Calories: 178
- Fat: 1 g
- Saturated Fat: 0 g
- Carbohydrates:47 g
- Fiber: 3 g
- Sodium: 3 mg
- Protein: 2 g

Grilled Eggplant

Prep Time: 10 minutes
Cooking Time: 10 minutes
Serving: 4

Ingredients:

- 2 small eggplants, half-inch slices
- 1/4 cup olive oil
- 2 tablespoons lime juice
- 3 teaspoons Cajun seasoning

Directions:

1. Liberally season the eggplant slices with oil, lemon juice, and Cajun seasoning.
2. Prepare and preheat the Ninja Foodi Grill on the medium temperature setting.
3. Once it is preheated, open the lid and place the eggplant slices in the grill.
4. Cover the Ninja Foodi Grill's lid and grill on the "Grilling Mode" for 5 minutes per side.
5. Serve.

Nutritional Values (Per Serving):

- Calories 372
- Total Fat 11.1 g
- Saturated Fat 5.8 g
- Cholesterol 610 mg
- Sodium 749 mg
- Total Carbs 16.9 g
- Fiber 0.2 g
- Sugar 0.2 g
- Protein 13.5 g

Crispy Crunchy Broccoli Delight

Prep Time: 5-10 minutes

Cooking Time: 15 minutes

Servings: 3

Ingredients:

- Lemon wedges
- 2 tablespoons parmesan, grated
- Salt and pepper to taste
- 2 tablespoons extra virgin olive oil
- 1 large broccoli head, cut into florets
- ¼ cup toasted almonds, sliced
- ½ teaspoon red pepper flakes

Directions:

1. Take a medium bowl and add broccoli, toss with olive oil
2. Season well with salt and pepper
3. Add pepper flakes for heat
4. Pre-heat your Ninja Foodi Grill in AIR CRISP mode to 390 degrees F, and set the timer to 15 minutes
5. Once you hear the beep, arrange a reversible trivet in Grill Pan
6. Arrange broccoli and roast until the timer is out
7. Serve with some cheese on top and the lemon wedges on the side
8. Enjoy!

Nutritional Values (Per Serving):

- Calories: 181
- Fat: 11 g
- Saturated Fat: 3 g
- Carbohydrates: 9 g
- Fiber: 4 g
- Sodium: 421 mg
- Protein: 8 g

Avocado Fries

Prep Time: 10 minutes
Cooking Time: 10 minutes
Servings: 4

Ingredients:

- 1/2 cup all-purpose flour
- 1-1/2 teaspoons pepper
- 2 eggs
- 1 tablespoon water
- 1/2 cup panko
- 2 avocados
- Cooking spray
- 1/4 teaspoon kosher salt

Directions:

1. Cut the avocado into 8 wedges each.
2. Beat the eggs and water in a bowl. Combine the flour and pepper in another bowl.
3. Place the panko on a plate. Toss the avocado wedges in flour, dip them in egg, and then dredge them through the panko.
4. Spray each wedge with cooking spray and transfer it to the basket.
5. Cook wedges in the Ninja Foodi Grill's AIR CRISP at 390°F for 10 minutes, tossing at least once.
6. Sprinkle with salt and serve.

Nutritional Values (Per Serving):

- Calories: 349
- Fiber: 8 g
- Fat: 22.7 g
- Carbs: 31 g
- Protein: 8.2 g.

Delicious Broccoli and Arugula

Prep Time: 10 minutes

Cooking Time: 12 minutes

Servings: 4

Ingredients:

- Pepper as needed
- ½ teaspoon salt
- Red pepper flakes
- 2 tablespoons extra virgin olive oil
- 1 tablespoon canola oil
- ½ red onion, sliced
- 1 garlic cloves, minced
- 1 teaspoon Dijon mustard
- 1 teaspoon honey
- 1 tablespoon lemon juice
- 2 tablespoons parmesan cheese, grated
- 4 cups arugula, torn
- 2 heads broccoli, trimmed

Directions:

1. Pre-heat your Ninja Foodi Grill to MAX and set the timer to 12 minutes
2. Take a large-sized bowl and add broccoli, sliced onion, and canola oil, toss the mixture well until coated
3. Once you hear the beep, it is pre-heated
4. Arrange your vegetables over the grill grate, let them grill for 8-12 minutes
5. Take a medium-sized bowl and whisk in lemon juice, olive oil, mustard, honey, garlic, red pepper flakes, pepper, and salt
6. Once done, add the prepared veggies and arugula in a bowl
7. Drizzle the prepared vinaigrette on top, sprinkle a bit of parmesan
8. Stir and mix
9. Enjoy!

Nutritional Values (Per Serving):

- Calories: 168
- Fat: 12 g
- Saturated Fat: 3 g
- Carbohydrates: 13 g
- Fiber: 1 g
- Sodium: 392 mg
- Protein: 6 g

Great Onion Rings

Prep Time: 10 minutes
Cooking Time: 10 minutes
Servings: 4

Ingredients:

- ¼ teaspoon salt
- 1 egg
- ¾ cup milk
- 1 tablespoon baking powder
- ¾ cup breadcrumbs
- 1 large onion
- 1 cup flour
- 1 teaspoon paprika

Directions:

1. Pre-heat Ninja Foodi by pressing the "AIR CRISP" option and setting it to "340 Degrees F" and timer to 10 minutes
2. let it pre-heat until you hear a beep
3. Take a bowl and whisk the egg, milk, salt, flour, paprika together
4. Slice the onion and separate into rings
5. Grease your Ninja Foodi Grill with cooking spray
6. Then dip the onion rings into batter and coat with breadcrumbs
7. Arrange them in Ninja Foodi Grill Cooking Basket
8. Cook for 10 minutes
9. Serve and enjoy!

Nutritional Values (Per Serving):

- Calories: 450
- Fat: 13 g
- Saturated Fat: 4 g
- Carbohydrates: 56 g
- Fiber: 6 g
- Sodium: 803 mg
- Protein: 30 g

Italian Spiced Squash

Prep Time: 5-10 minutes

Cooking Time: 16 minutes

Servings: 4

Ingredients:

- ¼ teaspoon black pepper
- 1 and ½ teaspoon dried oregano
- 1 tablespoon olive oil
- ½ teaspoon salt
- 1 teaspoon dried thyme
- 1 medium butternut squash, peeled and seeded, cut into ½ inch slices

Directions:

1. Take a mixing bowl and add listed ingredients alongside the slices, mix
2. Pre-heat your Ninja Foodi Grill to MED, setting the timer to 16 minutes
3. Once you hear the beep, arrange squash over the griller
4. Cook for 8 minutes, flip them over and cook for 8 minutes more
5. Serve and enjoy once done!

Nutritional Values (Per Serving):

- Calories: 238
- Fat: 12 g
- Saturated Fat: 2 g
- Carbohydrates: 36 g
- Fiber: 3 g
- Sodium: 128 mg
- Protein: 15 g

Crispy Potato Cubes

Prep Time: 10 minutes
Cooking Time: 20 minutes
Servings: 4

Ingredients:

- 1-pound potato, peeled
- 1 tablespoon olive oil
- 1 teaspoon dried dill
- 1 teaspoon dried oregano
- ¼ teaspoon chili flakes

Directions:

1. Pre-heat Ninja Foodi by pressing the "AIR CRISP" option and setting it to "400 Degrees F" and timer to 20 minutes
2. let it pre-heat until you hear a beep
3. Cut potatoes into cubes
4. Sprinkle potato cubes with dill, oregano and chili flakes
5. Transfer to Foodi Grill and cook for 15 minutes
6. Stir while cooking, once they are crunchy
7. Serve and enjoy!

Nutritional Values (Per Serving):

- Calories: 119
- Fat: 4 g
- Saturated Fat: 1 g
- Carbohydrates: 20 g
- Fiber: 3 g
- Sodium: 370 mg
- Protein: 12 g

Broccoli and Arugula Salad

Prep Time: 10 minutes
Cooking Time: 12 minutes
Servings: 4

Ingredients:

- 2 heads broccoli, trimmed into florets
- 4 cups arugula, torn
- 2 tablespoons parmesan cheese, grated
- 1 tablespoon lemon juice
- 1 teaspoon honey
- 1 teaspoon Dijon mustard
- 1 garlic clove, minced
- ½ red onion, sliced
- 1 tablespoon canola oil
- 2 tablespoons extra-virgin olive oil
- Red pepper flakes
- ¼ teaspoon of sea salt
- Black pepper, freshly grounded

Directions:

1. Supplement the flame broil mesh and close the hood
2. Pre-heat Ninja Foodi by pressing the "GRILL" option at and setting it to "MAX" and timer to 12 minutes
3. Take a large bowl and combine the broccoli, sliced onions, canola oil
4. Toss until coated
5. Once it pre-heat until you hear a beep
6. Arrange the vegetables over the grill grate, lock lid and cook for 8 to 12 minutes
7. Take a medium bowl and whisk together lemon juice, mustard, olive oil, honey, garlic, red pepper flakes, salt, and pepper
8. Once cooked, combine the roasted vegetables and arugula in a large serving bowl
9. Drizzle with the vinaigrette to taste and sprinkle with parmesan cheese
10. Serve and enjoy!

Nutritional Values (Per Serving):

- Calories: 168
- Fat: 12 g
- Saturated Fat: 3 g
- Carbohydrates: 13 g
- Fiber: 1 g
- Sodium: 392 mg
- Protein: 6 g

Roast Carrot and Cumin

Prep Time: 10 minutes
Cooking Time: 12 minutes
Servings: 4

Ingredients:

- 21 ounces carrots, peeled
- 1 tablespoon olive oil
- 1 teaspoon cumin seeds
- Handful fresh coriander

Directions:

1. Pre-heat Ninja Foodi by pressing the "AIR CRISP" option and setting it to "350 Degrees F" and timer to 12 minutes
2. let it pre-heat until you hear a beep
3. Take a mixing bowl and add oil, honey, and carrots
4. Give it a nice stir and make sure that they are coated well
5. Season with some dill, pepper, and salt
6. Transfer the mix to your Ninja Foodi Grill and cook for 12 minutes and enjoy it!

Nutritional Values (Per Serving):

- Calories: 210
- Fat: 5 g
- Saturated Fat: 1 g
- Carbohydrates: 5 g
- Fiber: 2 g
- Sodium: 450 mg
- Protein: 4 g

Chapter 7: Desserts, Bread & Rolls

Fiery Cajun Eggplant Dish

Prep Time: 5-10 minutes

Cooking Time: 12 minutes

Servings: 4

Ingredients:

- 2 tablespoons lime juice
- 3 teaspoons Cajun seasoning
- 2 small eggplants, cut into slices
- ¼ cup olive oil

Directions:

1. Coat eggplant slices with oil, lemon juice, and Cajun seasoning
2. Take your Ninja Foodi Grill and press "GRILL" and set to "MED" mode, set the timer to 10 minutes
3. Let it preheat
4. Arrange eggplants over grill grate, lock lid and cook for 5 minutes
5. Flip and cook for 5 minutes more
6. Serve and enjoy!

Nutritional Values (Per Serving):

- Calories: 362
- Fat: 11 g
- Saturated Fat: 3 g
- Carbohydrates: 16 g
- Fiber: 1 g
- Sodium: 694 mg
- Protein: 8 g

Chocolate Brownies

Prep Time: 15 minutes
Cooking time: 32 minutes
Servings: 4

Ingredients:

- 3 eggs
- ½ cup butter
- ½ cup sugar-free chocolate chips
- 2 scoops stevia
- 1 teaspoon vanilla extract

Directions:

1. Take a bowl and mix eggs, stevia, and vanilla extract.
2. Pour this mixture in the blender and blend until smooth.
3. Put the butter and chocolate in the pot of Ninja Foodi and press sauté.
4. Sauté for 2 minutes until the chocolate is melted.
5. Add the melted chocolate into the egg mixture.
6. Pour the mixture in the baking mold and place it in the Ninja Foodi.
7. Press "Bake" and set the timer for about 30 minutes at 360 degrees F.
8. Bake for about 30 minutes, cut into pieces and serve.

Nutritional Values (Per Serving):

- Calories 266
- Total Fat 26.9 g
- Saturated Fat 15.8 g
- Cholesterol 184 mg
- Sodium 218 mg
- Total Carbs 2.5 g
- Fiber 0 g
- Sugar 0.4 g
- Protein 4.5 g

The Healthy Granola Bites

Prep Time: 10 minutes

Cooking Time: 15-20 minutes

Servings: 4

Ingredients:

- Salt and pepper to taste
- 1 tablespoon coriander
- A handful of thyme, diced
- ¼ cup of coconut milk
- 3 handful of cooked vegetables, your choice
- 3 ounce plain granola

Directions:

1. Pre-heat your Ninja Foodi to 352 degrees F in AIR CRISP mode, set a timer to 20 minutes
2. Take a bowl and add your cooked vegetables, granola
3. Use an immersion blender to blitz your granola until you have a nice breadcrumb-like consistency
4. Add coconut milk to the mix and mix until you have a nice firm texture
5. Use the mixture to make granola balls and transfer them to your Grill
6. Cook for 20 minutes
7. Serve and enjoy!

Nutritional Values (Per Serving):

- Calories: 140
- Fat: 10 g
- Saturated Fat: 3 g
- Carbohydrates: 14 g
- Fiber: 4 g
- Sodium: 215 mg
- Protein: 2 g

The Original Corn Biscuit

Prep time: 10 minutes

Cooking time: 15-20 minutes

Servings: 4

Ingredients:

- 2/3 cup buttermilk
- 1/3 cup vegetable shortening
- ½ teaspoon salt
- 2 and ½ teaspoon baking powder
- ½ cup yellow cornmeal
- 1 and ½ cups all-purpose flour, plus more

Directions:

1. In a large-sized bowl, take flour, cornmeal, baking powder, salt
2. Then respectively add shortening, until it is well-combined, cut into the flour mixture, and the dough resembles fine coarse meal
3. Onward add buttermilk and stir continually until moist
4. Press the "AIR CRISP" option and set this in "350 Degrees F" to pre-heat Ninja Foodi with a 15 minutes timer
5. Until you hear a beep, keep it in the pre-heat process
6. When it is done, take some flour, dust on a clean work surface until cohesive dough forms, knead the mixture on a floured surface
7. Through that dough, roll out in a thick form and cut with a 2-inch biscuit cutter
8. Grease well of your crisper basket, place 6-8 biscuits in the basket
9. Put into the Grill and bake for 12-15 minutes until golden brown
10. Take out biscuits from the basket and repeat with remaining dough
11. Serve and enjoy!

Nutrition Values (Per Serving):

- Calories: 265
- Fat: 12 g
- Carbohydrates: 34 g
- Protein: 5 g
- Sodium: 310 mg
- Fiber: 6 g
- Saturated Fat: 4 g

Peanut Butter Cups

Prep Time: 15 minutes
Cooking time: 30 minutes
Servings: 3

Ingredients:

- 1 cup butter
- ¼ cup heavy cream
- 2 ounces unsweetened chocolate
- ¼ cup peanut butter, separated
- 4 packets stevia

Directions:

1. Melt the peanut butter and butter in a bowl and stir well with unsweetened chocolate, stevia, and cream.
2. Mix well and pour the mixture in a baking mold.
3. Put the baking mold in the Ninja Foodi and press "Bake"
4. Set the timer for 30 minutes at 360 degrees F and dish out to serve.

Nutritional Values (Per Serving):

- Calories 479
- Total Fat 51.5 g
- Saturated Fat 29.7 g
- Cholesterol 106 mg
- Sodium 69 mg
- Total Carbs 7.7 g
- Fiber 2.7 g
- Sugar 1.4 g
- Protein 5.2 g

Lovely Rum Sundae

Prep Time: 10 minutes

Cooking Time: 8 minutes

Servings: 4

Ingredients:

- Vanilla ice cream for serving
- 1 pineapple, cored and sliced
- 1 teaspoon cinnamon, ground
- ½ cup brown sugar, packed
- ½ cup dark rum

Directions:

1. Take a large deep bowl and add sugar, cinnamon, and rum
2. Add the pineapple in the layer, dredge them properly and make sure that they are coated well
3. Pre-heat your Foodi in "GRILL" mode with "MAX" settings, setting the timer to 8 minutes
4. Once you hear the beep, strain any additional rum from the pineapple slices and transfer them to the grill rate of your appliance
5. Press them down and grill for 6- 8 minutes. Make sure to not overcrowd the grill grate, cook in batches if needed
6. Top each of the ring with a scoop of your favorite ice cream, sprinkle a bit of cinnamon on top
7. Enjoy!

Nutritional Values (Per Serving):

- Calories: 240
- Fat: 4 g
- Saturated Fat: 1 g
- Carbohydrates: 43 g
- Fiber: 8 g
- Sodium: 85 mg
- Protein: 2 g

Mozzarella Sticks and Grilled Eggplant

Prep Time: 10 minutes

Cooking Time: 14 minutes

Servings: 4

Ingredients:

- Salt as needed
- ½ pound buffalo mozzarella, sliced into ¼ inch thick
- 12 large basil leaves
- 2 heirloom tomatoes, sliced into ¼ inch thickness
- 2 tablespoon canola oil
- 1 eggplant, ¼ inch thick

Directions:

1. Take a large bowl and add the eggplant, add oil and toss well until coated well
2. Pre-heat your Ninja Foodi to MAX and set the timer to 15 minutes
3. Once you hear the beeping sound, transfer the prepared eggplants to your Grill and cook for 8-12 minutes until the surface is charred
4. Top with cheese slice, tomato, and mozzarella
5. Cook for 2 minutes, letting the cheese melt
6. Remove from grill and place 2-3 basil leaves on top of half stack
7. Place remaining eggplant stack on top alongside basil
8. Season well with salt and rest of the basil
9. Enjoy!

Nutritional Values (Per Serving):

- Calories:
- Fat: 19 g
- Saturated Fat: 19 g
- Carbohydrates: 11 g
- Fiber: 4 g
- Sodium: 1555 mg
- Protein: 32 g

Flattering Banana Chips

Prep time: 5-10 minutes

Cooking time: 15 minutes

Servings: 4

Ingredients:

- 1 teaspoon olive oil
- ½ teaspoon Chaat Masala
- ½ teaspoon turmeric powder
- 1 teaspoon salt
- 3-4 raw banana

Directions:

1. Pre-heat your Ninja Foodi to 352 degrees F, in AIR CRISP mode, set the timer to 15 minutes
2. Peel the skin off the bananas, keep them on the side
3. Take a bowl and add salt, powder, turmeric, water
4. Cut banana slices into the mix, soak for 10 minutes
5. Drain the chips and dry them
6. Add a bit of oil on top
7. Transfer them to Ninja Grill basket and Grill for 15 minutes
8. Serve and enjoy!

Nutrition Values (Per Serving):

- Calories: 305
- Fat: 14 g
- Saturated Fat: 3 g
- Carbohydrates: 30 g
- Fiber: 3 g
- Sodium: 164 mg
- Protein: 4 g

Granola Flavored Healthy Muffin

Prep Time: 10 minutes

Cooking Time: 15-20 minutes

Servings: 4

Ingredients:

- 3 ounces plain granola
- 3 handful of cooked vegetables of your choice
- ¼ cup of coconut milk
- A handful of thyme diced
- 1 tablespoon coriander
- Salt and pepper to taste

Directions:

1. Preheat Ninja Foodi by pressing the "AIR CRISP" option and setting it to "352 Degrees F" and timer to 20 minutes
2. Take a mixing bowl and add cooked vegetables
3. Take an immersion blender and whiz granola until you have a breadcrumb-like texture
4. Add coconut milk to the granola and add veggies
5. Mix well into muffin/ball shapes
6. Transfer them to preheated Ninja Foodi Grill and cook for 20 minutes
7. Serve and enjoy once done!

Nutritional Values (Per Serving):

- Calories: 140
- Fat: 10 g
- Saturated Fat: 3 g
- Carbohydrates: 14 g
- Fiber: 4 g
- Sodium: 215 mg
- Protein: 2 g

Rummy Pineapple Sunday

Prep Time: 10 minutes

Cooking Time: 8 minutes

Servings: 4

Ingredients:

- ½ cup dark rum
- ½ cup packed brown sugar
- 1 teaspoon ground cinnamon, plus more for garnish
- 1 pineapple cored and sliced
- Vanilla ice cream, for serving

Directions:

1. Take a large-sized bowl and add rum, sugar, cinnamon
2. Add pineapple slices, arrange them in the layer. Coat mixture then let them soak for 5 minutes, per side
3. Preheat Ninja Foodi by pressing the "GRILL" option and setting it to "MAX" and timer to 8 minutes
4. let it preheat until you hear a beep
5. Strain extra rum sauce from pineapple
6. Transfer prepared fruit in grill grate in a single layer, press down fruit and lock lid
7. Grill for 6-8 minutes without flipping, work in batches if needed
8. Once done, remove and top each pineapple ring with a scoop of ice cream, sprinkle cinnamon and serve
9. Enjoy!

Nutritional Values (Per Serving):

- Calories: 240
- Fat: 4 g
- Saturated Fat: 2 g
- Carbohydrates: 43 g
- Fiber: 3 g
- Sodium: 32 mg
- Protein: 2 g

Premium Tomato and Bacon Omelet

Prep time: 5-10 minutes

Cooking time: 10 minutes

Servings: 4

Ingredients:

- Salt and pepper to taste
- 1 tablespoon olive oil
- 1 tablespoon parsley, chopped
- 4 tomatoes, cubed
- ¼ pound cubed, cooked, and chopped
- 1 tablespoon cheddar, grated
- 4 whole eggs, whisked

Directions:

1. Take a small-sized pan and place it over medium heat, add bacon and Saute for 2 minutes until crispy
2. Take a bowl and add bacon, alongside the remaining ingredients
3. Stir well, sprinkle cheese on top
4. Pre-heat your Ninja Foodi to 400 degrees F in BAKE mode, set timer to 10 minutes
5. Pour mixture into a baking dish, transfer baking dish to Ninja Foodi Grill
6. Bake for 8 minutes
7. Serve and enjoy!

Nutrition Values (Per Serving):

- Calories: 311
- Fat: 16 g
- Saturated Fat: 4 g
- Carbohydrates: 23 g
- Fiber: 4 g
- Sodium: 149 mg
- Protein: 22 g

Great Mac and Cheese Bowl

Prep Time: 10 minutes

Cooking Time: 10 minutes

Servings: 4

Ingredients:

- 1 tablespoon parmesan cheese, grated
- Salt and pepper to taste
- 1 and ½ cup cheddar cheese, grated
- ½ cup warm milk
- ½ cup broccoli
- 1 cup elbow macaroni

Directions:

1. Pre-heat your Ninja Foodi to 400 degrees F in AIR CRISP mode, set a timer to 10 minutes
2. Once you hear the beep, it is pre-heated
3. Take a pot and add water, bring the water to a boil
4. Add macaroni and veggies, boil for 10 minutes until cooked
5. Drain pasta and veggies, toss pasta and veggies with cheese and sauce
6. Season well with salt and pepper and transfer to Ninja Foodi
7. Sprinkle more cheese on top and cook for 15 minutes
8. Take it out and let it cool for 10 minutes
9. Serve and enjoy!

Nutritional Values (Per Serving):

- Calories: 180
- Fat: 11 g
- Saturated Fat: 3 g
- Carbohydrates: 14 g
- Fiber: 3 g
- Sodium: 287 mg
- Protein: 6 g

Marshmallow Banana Boat

Prep Time: 19 minutes

Cooking Time: 6 minutes

Servings: 4

Ingredients:

- 4 ripe bananas
- 1 cup mini marshmallows
- ½ cup of chocolate chips
- ½ cup peanut butter chips

Directions:

1. Slice a banana lengthwise, keeping its peel. Make sure to not cut all the way through

2. Use your hands to open banana peel like a book, revealing the inside of a banana

3. Divide marshmallow, chocolate chips, peanut butter among bananas, stuffing them inside

4. Preheat Ninja Foodi by pressing the "GRILL" option and setting it to "MEDIUM" and timer to 6 minutes

5. let it preheat until you hear a beep

6. Transfer banana to Grill Grate and lock lid, cook for 4-6 minutes until chocolate melts and bananas are toasted

7. Serve and enjoy!

Nutritional Values (Per Serving):

- Calories: 505
- Fat: 18 g
- Saturated Fat: 13 g
- Carbohydrates: 82 g
- Fiber: 6 g
- Sodium: 103 mg
- Protein: 10 g

CPSIA information can be obtained
at www.ICGtesting.com
Printed in the USA
BVHW020306190523
664477BV00004BA/29

To my wife and best friend, Michelle.

There is no one else I want to be on this ride with.
You inspire me every day.

SECOND CHANCE CEO

HOW CRISES MADE ME A BETTER LEADER, MENTOR AND COACH

TOM CAPORASO

SECOND CHANCE CEO
How Crises Made Me a Better Leader, Mentor and Coach

ISBN   HARDCOVER: 978-1-5445-3259-2
       PAPERBACK: 978-1-5445-3258-5
       EBOOK: 978-1-5445-3257-8

CONTENTS

INTRODUCTION

Every morning when I look in the bathroom mirror, I see the long scar that stretches right down the middle of my chest like a rough zipper.

I was twenty-nine years old when the surgeon cut me open, cracked my sternum, and performed open-heart surgery. That was over two decades ago. I hadn't even been aware of a problem with my heart. It was only when a friend told me he was having a physical that I thought, "Well, I should probably get one, too."

I was reasonably fit. I was a young executive who worked hard and played hard; I'd not long before been inspired to complete a marathon by my dad, who was a runner. But the doctor said, "I think I hear a murmur. You'd better get it checked out." Then the specialist put a camera down my throat and said, "You've got a hole in your heart."

The quarter-sized hole was losing blood where it shouldn't. I needed open-heart surgery.

It's a scary thing, being told your body might kill you. It knocks you off your stride. It also makes you question what you want to achieve and where you want to be—and how you're going to get there.

You can't help but look at what you're doing and wonder if you're doing it right. Or even if you're doing the right thing at all.

I wasn't unreasonably worried. I had enough time before the operation to get into better shape, and I knew that would help my rehab. But I couldn't avoid concluding that I wasn't as indestructible as I thought.

Pivot Point

In my late twenties, I was 100 percent sure nothing could stop me. I was dating the woman who became my wife. I was moving up in my work and telling my bosses whenever I got the chance that I could go higher, quicker. I was a hard-charging guy with a clear career path mapped out in my head that led to the C-suite and the CEO's office.

I was impatient to get there.

It felt as if I was treading water, as if everything I was doing was going through the motions. It was just the downtime that was necessary before I could move on to the next stage.

I wasn't living in the present because in my mind I was already rushing ahead into the future. What I was doing in my career wasn't as important as where it would lead me next.

But sometimes when you think you're going along fine, life kicks you in the gut.

You've got a good job, you're rising up through the business—albeit a bit slower than you'd like—and you've got excellent prospects. You're in decent physical and mental shape. Your finances are looking good. Maybe you're settling down, having kids, raising a family. You're growing into the future you've imagined for yourself.

Then—bam!—you're laid out on an operating table, your life in someone else's hands, unable to think straight and barely able to catch your breath.

I recovered quickly after the surgery. I was up on my feet the day after the operation and back in the office after about three weeks. Today, my heart is fine and I'm fit and active.

But every morning when I get up and start thinking about the day ahead, I see the scar bisecting my torso.

That scar reminds me that there are bigger things to worry about than what's going on in the office, what stage my career is at, or how close I am to another raise.

It reminds me that I'd better get something good out of today rather than wasting it looking forward to a future that might not happen.

That's what open-heart surgery, or any medical scare, does. It's a stark reminder that there's not always a tomorrow.

Only an idiot would ignore a warning like that.

Open-heart surgery divided my life into two clear phases: before the operation and after it. Or what I sometimes call Tom 1.0 and Tom 2.0

Surgery forced me to reconsider my attitude toward myself, my family, my friends, and my work.

Second Chance

A lot of people will tell you that there are no second chances. They're usually exactly the sort of hard chargers I was when I was younger. They tell you that if you don't grab the chance *now*, it's gone. I'd likely have told you the same thing.

I would have been wrong. And *they're* wrong. I became a

2.0 version of myself, with bugs removed and enhancements added. I got a second chance.

It made me a better person. A better partner, a better friend, a better worker...and now a better CEO. Being wheeled into the operating theater on that gurney taught me more about being an effective manager than any number of years at my desk or in meetings.

It would be exaggerating to call it a near-death experience—in fact, I was serenely confident throughout that I would come through the surgery fine, which probably says more about my attitude at the time than about the seriousness of the operation—but it had a similar effect.

I got to hit "reset." I got to take a look at myself and decide what was important to me: where I was going, what I was doing, and how I was doing it.

I shifted my priorities. For years after the operation, whenever I had to do a big presentation or anything else that made me nervous, I wrote in big letters across the top of the front page "OHS."

Open-heart surgery.

Those three letters reminded me that, however intimidated I might be by whatever I was slated to do, it wasn't that serious. It couldn't go that badly wrong. It didn't threaten my very existence. It didn't even deserve any undue fear. In the great scheme of things, it's likely not even a footnote.

Crisis #2

Those three letters gave me a sense of perspective. Just like my scar does every day. I'd learned a hell of a lesson.

As if that wasn't enough, a few years later I got the chance to learn the same lesson again. This time from Dr. Death.

Our twin daughters were born very prematurely. They needed constant attention just to keep them alive. They were left with serious medical conditions.

Enter Dr. Death.

That was what my wife and I named one clinician. Dr. Death took an extremely negative view. He didn't pass up any chance to tell us that the road to recovery would be long, and perhaps even endless. It would take many years before we could even tell how badly damaged the girls' bodies and brains might be.

I'm sure Dr. Death thought he was only being honest, but that's not what a parent wants to hear when their heart is broken and they're trying to put it back together.

That was a new lesson. That just because something might be true doesn't give you the right to say it, or at least not to say it without regard for how others will take it.

That's what I used to be like, in my original version. I was sometimes guilty of believing that being brutally direct meant I was somehow being more effective at communication. I was more concerned with achieving goals than with having empathy for my colleagues.

I wasn't alone. That attitude is common in corporate America. It excuses all kinds of communication that is so direct it's almost rude. But brutal honesty is not always the best policy.

Just ask my wife and me back when we were sitting in that hospital room with our twins while Dr. Death kept reminding us not just that everything was truly awful but that it likely wouldn't get any better.

Believe Me, It's a Virtue

In the early part of my career, I felt I was constantly getting stuck. Advancement wasn't coming quickly enough, at least not in the opinion of someone who was pretty full of his own abilities.

It never occurred to me that I might not have the experience or skills to move up. I just couldn't get there fast enough.

I recognize my former self in many middle managers and junior executives I meet today. They are hungry for advancement and can't see why their career isn't happening quicker. They know that something is blocking their rise, but they don't know what it is. They don't understand why the rewards they were expecting remain out of reach.

I tell them the best advice I know. Be patient.

They treat that advice exactly how I would have treated it in the past. They ignore it completely.

Just as I would have done, they think that being patient means being passive. That it means resigning yourself simply to wait for the next opportunity. Nothing could be further from the truth.

Being patient in your professional life isn't about abandoning your ambitions. It still means working hard and learning, and aiming for advancement. But it also means trusting that in time good things will happen if you play your part. Most importantly, it is a way of reminding yourself to enjoy whatever stage you're at.

The best way to find success in business is to enjoy the journey rather than obsessing with reaching the final destination as quickly as possible.

That might not be a particularly profound lesson, but it changed my life—and it can change yours.

I learned the hard way. I had my surgery. I held my wife while we sat in a dark, timeless place while our girls' lives balanced on a knife edge.

I want to show you the lessons I've learned *without* you having to go through the same traumatic experiences I went through.

I want you to gain the benefits without carrying the scars.

I'll show you how I changed my attitude from one of an alpha male pursuing the C-suite at all costs to himself and those around him to a more holistic approach based on patience, tolerance, and getting my priorities right.

In Action

Today, I run ebbo™, recently renamed from Clarus Commerce, which we built into one of the country's biggest providers of loyalty programs for companies of all sizes.

When I joined Clarus—my first job as a CEO—we had ten employees. We grew almost constantly to around 170, when we made an acquisition that doubled that number and opened the way to the creation of the two go-to-market brands. I've sold the company three times to different investors. I've learned constantly since the first day I walked through the doors until the pandemic arrived in spring 2020. If the board of directors is happy, the team is happy—and I'm happy.

Above all, everyone is healthy—including me, and including the twins.

I still believe that's the most important thing of all. How could I not, given my experiences? But that doesn't mean that

I'm not focused on performance, getting results, and building the business.

There's often an unspoken assumption in business that those two goals—happiness and performance—are mutually exclusive.

Not true.

Much of the company's success comes from its culture, and that starts with me as CEO.

I don't manage through fear. I don't like the idea of a CEO being a dictator. I've worked for bosses like that, and I didn't appreciate them. Managing through fear may bring short-term results, but ultimately it's going to leave employees weary and miserable. And you hollowed out and frustrated.

That's no way to work. It's no way to live. And it's certainly no way to establish a sustainable work–life balance.

Sustainable meaning that, if you end up on a hospital gurney, you're content that you've got the attitude with which you approach your work right *and* you've got the way you approach your life right.

I thought I'd gotten it right when I was younger. It was only the surgery that brought me up short and made me reconsider.

That led me to focus on compassion and empathy—the very qualities I most valued from my bosses when I was at my lowest ebb. That has built into an emphasis on people.

Everyone says their most valuable asset is their people, I know. At ebbo™, it's the core of what we do. I value and solicit input, ideas, and suggestions from everyone. I give people time and room to grow, so they can gain experience with systems and decision-making at their current level before they can move up.

That's something I didn't understand in Version 1.0.

It's not that we don't want people to move up. It's just that sometimes the best way to help them move up is to hold them back while they get the tools and experience they need. That way, when they do move up, it's sustainable and solid—and more satisfying for them.

Empathy doesn't mean there are any easy rides. I work hard and I expect my team members to work hard. That's the only way to learn and grow so that you can take the next step.

If you think your job is the only thing that defines you, then you are going to get frustrated. You will be driven crazy just about every day. That's inevitable.

But if you realize work is simply a part of what makes you who you are—if you see that it is only one component of a life that includes your family and your relationships, as well as your mental and physical health—then you realize that you don't have to burn energy on being frustrated. You can take a step back and give yourself a chance of truly enjoying your work life as one part of everything you do. If you can find that balance and live it, work can be a source of pleasure and joy *while* you wait for whatever step comes next.

Avoid the Surgery

This book is a distillation of all I have learned about being the best CEO I can.

It takes all the lessons symbolized by the scar on my chest and lays them out on paper for other people to share.

In the following pages I will lay out a business philosophy based on empathy, fun, collaboration, learning, and teaching. I will show you through real-life experience how these ways of doing business lead to success and fulfillment for everyone involved.

This book is not a handbook or a single-destination guide with steps that take you from point A to point B. Nor is it an idealized rainbows-and-unicorns view of management where simply being nice to each other brings optimal results.

There is more to my philosophy of management than that. Hard work will bring results, but hard work is not the whole story. You need to start with the realization that good results and a good working environment go hand in hand.

You need to start with a strong commitment to creating a supportive and nurturing environment of teamwork and team building.

It's far easier to do that by turning to the next chapter than by undergoing major surgery or emotional trauma. So let's go!

CHAPTER 1

TEAM
PHILOSOPHY

M ost companies put on a good show for a new hire. They get taken around and introduced. Everyone's welcoming.

It doesn't always last much beyond the first day. A lot of workplaces are like dog-fighting pits. Everyone's baring their teeth and snarling at anyone they think might get ahead.

I've worked in places like that.

I used to revel in the competition. Now I just find it insane. What a crazy waste of energy and time. What an appalling way to treat other people. What a self-centered way to see the world.

I don't let it happen at ebbo™. I want team players, not alpha males or alpha females. No one climbs over anyone else to get ahead—and if they try, that's a surefire way of *not* getting ahead.

It's the same with me. I'm not some kind of CEO straight out of central casting who doesn't give a care about others, doesn't give his people the time of day, and sabotages their home lives by running them into the ground while he's strolling around on the golf course.

I've had bosses who reveled in their own power and deliberately set everyone else against one another, like they were courtiers at Versailles fighting for the king's attention. They managed by fear. It's never effective for long. Good people soon move on. No one can make worthwhile relationships with a boss like that, and relationships are what make a business thrive.

I hate being called a boss. I was brought up to hate the idea that any one person is more important than others. I don't have employees or associates; I have team members, and everyone is on the team. Including me. We share the same open floor plan. There is no C-suite.

Everything's in the open.

Trust the Players

It's a truism that a good business leader is like a good sports manager.

The parallels are clear. Getting the right players, putting them together in the most effective teams, drilling them on their plays, making sure they know the tactics to effect the strategy.

There's another parallel. Once the players are on the field, there's only so much the manager can do. He or she has to trust them.

The easiest way to gain that trust is to make sure the team has the right tools and the right information.

All the information.

Four or five years ago we decided to share the company financials at our regular town hall meetings. All of them, good or bad.

A lot of CEOs might be resistant to that idea. If the company's doing well, they'd be concerned that everyone might start asking for raises, or start sitting back on the job. If the company's doing badly, they'd be concerned that everyone would start finding new places to work.

They're both risks I was prepared to accept. In the end, there was nothing to worry about. The overwhelming reaction wasn't greed or concern: it was gratitude for being trusted with the information.

For being allowed to know what goes on under the hood, behind closed doors, in leadership meetings.

To know what I know.

Every Monday I have a team meeting with my eight direct reports. As soon as it's over we publish the notes of the meeting to the entire company. Everyone is aware of what's going on. Everyone is empowered to read the notes and go execute for themselves.

I go further, too. As part of the financial presentation, I do a slide show called Wins and Struggles. We highlight all the great things that we achieved, but we also share the places where we have to get better: goals missed, challenges not quite met, results less than hoped for.

Part of it is often a *mea culpa* by me. I stand up in front of the whole company and give them a list of my own mistakes through the year. The bad hires. The products that didn't quite happen. The opportunities not fully exploited. I say, "Jeez, I swung and I missed, and that had an impact on you all."

That sort of admission builds trust. You can't have an effective team without transparency, and you can't have transparency without sharing the good and the bad. If you only share good things, no one's going to believe you, because they're not idiots. And if you only share bad things, no one's going to want to work for you, because they'll lose their morale.

There's another word for this approach to team-building anyone can relate to. It's not some fancy management speak out of a manual. It's called honesty.

Tell the Truth

Tell the truth and be true to yourself.

The same thing I tell my kids—the same thing you tell your kids—is how you build your strongest team. By setting an example where everyone tells the truth and knows that whatever they hear is the truth, too. That way everyone develops trust. That way, everyone is free to be authentically themselves.

A few years ago, the company faced a huge blow out of nowhere. Maybe not terminal, but potentially massively damaging to the bottom line, and therefore to our growth and our continued investment.

We had partnered with a large advertising partner for years. We promoted one of our products, freeshipping.com, on their site. It was one of our biggest revenue streams. Then one day, out of the blue, the partner decided to create their own shipping product, similar to Amazon Prime—and similar to freeshipping .com.

Not only were we going to lose access to their site, but now that we were in direct competition with them. The decision came in November, right before the holiday shopping season. There couldn't be a worse time to lose so much business.

They had killed the goose. No more golden eggs.

The first thing we did was to tell the whole team. That wouldn't have happened in many firms. A lot of businesses react to crises by keeping them within as small a team as possible to avoid panic.

We told everyone. We told them that we'd lost a big revenue generator. We told them it was the worst possible timing. We told them the bottom line would take a hell of a hit. And we told them that we desperately needed a new product to replace what we'd lost.

The result was Shop Smarter, a new product that didn't involve any shipping element. That meant our partner would let us back on the site.

Better still, we had the product up and running sixty days after we had the idea. I can't remember a quicker turnaround.

The only way we could do that was because the whole team pitched in. Shop Smarter was all hands on deck. It wasn't in anyone's job description, but everybody pitched in.

They understood the stakes. They knew we weren't bluffing about the blow we'd taken.

So they were motivated to work their butts off.

When you tell your team exactly what's going on, they *want* to make things work.

Getting Clarity

It was the same when the pandemic struck in spring 2020.

Everyone was worried and nothing was clear. There was no

timetable, no structure, no stability. Everyone was worried for themselves and their families. For their communities. For the whole country.

Part of my job was putting the team's minds at ease.

I was completely truthful. I told them that there was lots I didn't know. Honestly, there was more I didn't know than I did. I told them we had money in the bank, so we had some short-term security. I told them we were talking to all our clients so they knew what was happening. And I told them that we were looking at the broader picture of what was happening in America.

I didn't promise that everyone would keep their job, because I couldn't. But I did tell them that our goal was to not lay anybody off. That was a relief to team members whose partners had just lost their jobs.

We sent everyone to work from home for two weeks. Then a few months. And eventually over a year and a half.

We overcommunicated. We used emails, town halls, and videos to reach out to everyone. I checked in with groups and individuals at every level. I asked how they were doing. How was their family? How were their kids?

These check-ins became a key part of my job. I'd do five or ten calls each week during the pandemic as a way to let the team know that the company cared about them.

That I cared about them.

I'll talk later about exactly how we navigated the pandemic, but the key result here is this. We kept everyone together. We kept their spirits up, their work stimulating, and their salaries paid. We didn't lose a single team member.

Lose the Ego

It's easy for people moving up in their career to become too impressed by themselves. They get promoted for a reason and it goes to their heads.

I used to stick my chest out as I strode through the office. Then someone took a knife and cut it open.

That keeps you humble.

Pride has a place in any team; it's a fantastic motivator. Arrogance has no place. It kills team spirit.

Pride comes not from your own valuation of yourself but from that of others. At our town halls, team members can call out a coworker for doing a great job or going the extra mile. It's effective because it's recognition from your peers—and they know exactly what it takes to do good work.

Once a year the whole team votes on a series of awards: Most Valuable Player, Rookie of the Year, and Unsung Hero.

I get one vote, like everyone else. Though I did create my own award, the Spotlight Award, where I get my own choice of someone whose contribution I want to highlight.

Arrogance is thinking you're better than someone else. Or perhaps than everyone else. It's just as bad if it's justified as if it isn't.

An environment where everyone is fighting for rank makes arrogance an easy habit to fall into.

We sometimes have outside hires who look around for an assistant to open their mail or make them a coffee.

We open our own mail. We make our own coffee.

Everyone pitches in and works. Including me. Humility is a quality people respond to in leaders.

When I was younger I had some bosses who were idiots. They managed through negativity. They put everyone down except themselves.

I would have preferred to be managed by someone like me. Or at least by me as I am today. I'm fair and balanced and direct, and you always know where I stand. If you did a good job, you'll know it; and if you did a bad job, you'll know it too. All in real time.

It's never purely negative. It's always supportive. And that helps create an environment that becomes self-sustaining.

Teamwork is built into the system. It doesn't only emerge when we're facing a crisis. It happened, for example, when an existing client purchased a new brand and asked us to build a new loyalty program.

Before we accepted, I shared the idea with the team. The client wanted to move fast, so it was going to put everyone under great pressure. They recognized the opportunity. They embraced it.

Again, we had it up and running in sixty days.

Again it was one of our top performers that year.

And again it owed its existence to team spirit.

Call the Plays

Fostering team spirit isn't the same as managing by committee. Everyone gets to have their say, but I make the calls.

In a company funded by growth equity, it's my head on the line if targets aren't met. That's why I sometimes say, "OK, I hear you, but now we're going to do it a different way." I let the team know where my decisions fit into the whole, but the buck stops where it always stops.

With the leader.

CHAPTER 2

LEAD BY EXAMPLE

One of the things I most enjoyed doing was coaching my son Tommy's baseball team. We practiced, we ran drills, we hung out. I liked to teach them that having fun and being involved is more important than winning.

It's a lesson some of the kids' parents never seem to have learned.

Another thing I taught the kids is that what we say matters. If you tell someone they can take a turn as pitcher or first baseman, let them have their turn—no matter how the game stands. If you shout for a catch, you'd better make it. If you tell your team you're going to play, then don't stay home because there's football on TV.

Words matter. No matter what you do in life, your words need to match up with your actions. Saying something you can't or don't follow up on shows that you're only talking a good game. You're not authentic.

It's the same in business. If I have a salesperson promise me she is going to land a big client, one that will help us prosper and grow, I accept her at her word. If she then doesn't do it, that calls her authenticity into question. On the other hand, if she tells me she worked hard on the proposal, anticipated all the questions she might get, and rehearsed her presentation, so she's ready to do her best, that I can respect and get behind, whether she wins the client or not.

I tell my own kids all the time that it is actions, not words, that gain you respect. It's the same with my team at ebbo™. You've got to follow through on what you say, so make sure your words match up with your actions.

Work–Life Balance

It's key to my business philosophy that I lead by example, not by words. I can talk the talk as well as anyone else, but a CEO or any other leader has to be able to walk the walk. Words that aren't followed up mean nothing.

I practice what I preach. If I want my team to do something, I set the example by doing it first. Including by not always putting work first.

When I faced my two life crises—my surgery and the premature birth of my daughters—I recalibrated my work–life balance.

I figured out what was important in my life, like spending time with family, and I took steps to make room for it. So when I encourage my team to figure out their own priorities in life, they know I'm being authentic.

Don't get me wrong. Work is important. It's a crucial part of our lives. But if the members of my team are spending all their time at work, or thinking about work, then something is wrong.

That used to be true of me in my life. I was all about work all the time until I learned the hard way that things don't have to be that way. I've got the scar on my chest to remind me. A fulfilling life includes work, of course, but it doesn't mean work takes up all my time or energy.

There are lots more things that make living worthwhile.

A Bad Hire

We all make mistakes. Let me tell you about one of my biggest.

A few years ago, we needed a chief technology officer. At the time we had two VPs running the technical side of the company but they left around the same time, so it was a logical decision to get a CTO who could take over that part of the operation and help us grow the business.

The person I hired came from within the industry. He had a good work history, and he was highly recommended. I was confident I'd made the right hire.

It soon turned out that I was wrong. The new CTO was not well-organized, and he didn't treat people well. He was nasty in one-on-one interactions. He was insulting, dismissive, and extremely negative.

Even worse, he was none of those things in front of me. It's one thing to be an abrasive personality, but if you modulate your natural abrasiveness to try to please the boss, then you're not being authentic. You're acting like a good guy in front of me and treating everyone else like shit. That's the worst kind of hypocrisy because it shows you *can* be a decent human being; you simply choose not to.

The other problem with the new guy was that he didn't achieve very much. He talked a lot of trash, but he didn't do a lot of anything. He blustered and boasted in meetings, then went away and didn't follow up.

I started getting negative feedback about the CTO very early on and I realized I'd made a mistake. I spoke to him and explained how we operated, and what kind of culture we liked to promote and champion. I encouraged him to get on board with our methods.

He never did. He was not representative of what I wanted the company to be, and he was dragging everyone else down. I let him go. I think he lasted about a hundred days.

At the end of the year, during our holiday party, I stood up in front of the entire team, every employee, and told them that the worst mistake I made that year was to hire that CTO. In telling them about my awful hire, I was leading by example. I was owning up to my mistake and letting everyone know that I was aware of the strain I put them under and how disruptive that CTO was to our team.

I believe that when I am wrong, I need to say I'm wrong. No evasions, no excuses. When I get it right, I get the slaps on the back. The flipside works, too. My mistake caused a lot of problems. It had a ripple effect not only on everyone in the organization but also to the team's families outside, and it impacted the bottom line of the business.

By letting everyone know I was aware of the consequences of my error, I hope I was showing the team that they could also own up to their mistakes without fear of the reaction. No one is perfect. No one. It's only by admitting errors and learning from them that we all get better, and we help build the team.

The worst thing about my mistake hiring the CTO was that I'd fallen for his BS. I hate people who are all talk. I don't tolerate them in the business. Our companies are built on honesty and authenticity. It took the rest of the team to see him for what he was.

I gave him the opportunity to improve, and he passed. So I fired him.

Leadership Doesn't Have to Mean Sacrifice

There is a popular image of a CEO as a hard-driving go-getter who sacrifices everything to his or her career. You see this in the popular media—in movies, television shows, and novels—male or female, young or old.

The hard-ass cares nothing for their employees or, for that matter, members of their own family. They make people work through the night or on Christmas. They have business drinks rather than going home for dinner. It's a cliché—and it's wrong.

It's what people who watch *The Apprentice* think is success in business.

I wasn't immune. I was like the cliché in many ways. Nothing was going to get in the way of me moving up the corporate ladder to the C-suite. The message I was giving out to everyone in my sphere was to get out of the way if they didn't want to get rolled over.

I was wrong. And the chances are that if you're like that, you're wrong too.

True leadership does not have to involve getting to work before everyone else and leaving after everyone else has gone. It can do, but it shouldn't. It does not mean putting in long hours at the expense of those you love. Again, it might do in an emergency, but it shouldn't. And it should never mean missing your daughter's concert or your son's baseball game in favor of a meeting to nail down a deal.

You're the leader. Reschedule.

That's what my experiences on the operating table or in the ICU waiting as the twins fought for their lives taught me. They made me change my priorities. I leave work early if there is an important family event. I encourage everyone else in the team to do the same. That's the way a true leader leads.

I'd never stop someone from leaving early. In fact, I'd actively encourage them to go. And it's not just because I want people to see me as a super-nice guy.

For one thing, I still expect the work to get done. If there are deadlines that need to be met, the person can come back to the office in the evening or they can come in early the next day. If that's not possible, we can get the team to cover. Or even the leadership team. Someone's got to do the work.

For another thing, a healthier work–life balance makes everyone happier, sharper, and more productive. By setting an example and letting them know that it is acceptable to have an enriching personal life, I help keep the team near its peak.

COVID Chaos

The work-life balance got thrown out for the whole world early in spring 2020, when the COVID-19 pandemic struck. Now it wasn't a question of doing one then the other. For many people, they were doing both at the same time, working from home while surrounded by kids, doing homeschooling, caring for seniors, getting supplies—and falling sick or convalescing.

It was a terrible time, of course. Working near people you had worked with for years became risky behavior.

As soon as things looked like they were going to be bad, we started to look at how we could reorganize the way we worked: setting up remote work schedules, getting everyone familiar with Zoom, and allowing flexible hours.

No one knew what would happen—and uncertainty is the enemy of any business. It certainly doesn't help people who are trying to protect and provide for their families while still doing a good job for their employers.

I tried to remain calm, to work the problem, and to keep a perspective on things. The business was important, but my family was even more so. I'd come close to losing two of them before: I wasn't putting anything above keeping them safe.

But a CEO has a second family to protect, and that's what I also tried to do. We started by listening carefully to our team members so we could understand what they needed from us. I spent a lot of time doing one-on-ones with my team from the early days, when half of them had never been on Zoom.

I wanted to let them know I was listening, and that I was open to suggestions.

Right from the start, we let people work from home. It's something a lot of companies resist, which I suspect is because they can't keep track of people at home. They can't tell how much of the day they spend working. My view is that it doesn't matter.

Why should I care if someone is playing with their kid for an hour in the middle of the day? I shouldn't. A CEO is entitled to care if the work gets done and deadlines are met—and nothing more.

More companies should adopt that approach. Everyone likes to be trusted.

Maternity Matters

In some ways, the pandemic helped us. By which I mean that it helped *me*. I think it made me a better CEO. It certainly encouraged better communication.

One of my one-on-ones was with a team member who had just come back from maternity leave. She asked me when I last reviewed our maternity leave program. I honestly couldn't remember.

It turned out I had not looked at it in years, and it was completely out of date. We rolled up our sleeves and dug into the program. We checked around to see what other companies were doing. We asked team members what they wanted from a maternity program. Then we did what they had asked. We made the program more supportive of both expectant and new mothers, and we added an entitlement to paternity leave.

Both were things we should have done a long time before, but they weren't anywhere near the top of my list of priorities.

To be truthful, they probably weren't even on the list at all. The changes only happened because we have a culture where people feel like they can come to the CEO and tell him where his company is falling down on the job of supporting his workers.

Because I tell people the truth, they feel they can tell me the truth. And speaking frankly allowed us all to discover places where we needed to improve our organization.

Being Authentic

There are days I don't look much like a CEO. When I'm in my T-shirt and shorts, you could mistake me for a janitor or a delivery man. We don't have a dress code because I don't believe you have to look like a professional to do a professional job.

I don't think how people look is important. All I ask is: Can you do the work? Can you do it well and on time? Can you consistently meet deadlines? Are you respectful, honest, and authentic?

I try to be exactly who I am everywhere, including in the office, and that extends to what I choose to wear. It's the same for everyone else. They can choose comfort or style or some combination of both. It's up to them. We should all be as authentic to ourselves as we can be.

The lack of a dress code isn't an invitation to wear dirty, provocative, or offensive clothes. That's a simple matter of respect, which is key to being professional.

Punctuality is another matter of respect. That's something I drum into my kids but a lot of people overlook that. Without punctuality, there can be no true trust. If people have to wait around for you to come to a meeting or turn in an important report, they can tell you think you're more important than they are.

Casual style does not mean casual work habits. It means being true to yourself and respecting others. That's always the bottom line.

PTSD

I rely on constant feedback. Listening to team members is the only way I can get to know what's really going on—like with the idiot CTO.

Sometimes new hires can't believe it when they walk in the door for the first time. They are used to workplaces in which there is naked ambition, backstabbing, toxic office politics, and dictatorial and unempathetic bosses. We set out to be the complete opposite.

The contrast with their old firms almost gives them a kind of PTSD. They're a bit overwhelmed and unsure what to do. They're not sure it's actually real.

We have to reassure them that it is.

And it's not because we're all softies. It's because being authentic, feeling supported in your family and personal life, and being part of a team you feel good about is the best way to achieve business success and to recruit and retain the best people.

A good leader balances work and life. A truly authentic leader sets the example. It's really very simple. We learn it as children. We don't necessarily do what our parents tell us to do, but we sure do what we see them doing.

It's no different in business. Action always trumps words. People do what they see you doing. The key is to model what you want to see around you: healthy work–life balance, empathy for others, team spirit, and authenticity.

In the next chapter we'll see how these qualities can spread from the CEO to the rest of the organization. It's all about empathy.

CHAPTER 3

MANAGE WITH EMPATHY

One day many years ago my daughter Tess fell off her bike. Like kids do, right? But Tess had been so premature that her stomach had had to be bypassed for some time, then reconnected. And the end of the bike handlebar had pierced right into the place where she'd had her operation. It was serious.

She had to have emergency surgery, so I had to take some days off.

Everyone at work was great about it. You'd hope they would be. What sort of colleague is going to make things more difficult for someone who's already having a bad time? And yet people do. People act as if they're only interested in work, or in the task. They think worrying about other people's problems or other people's feelings is a sign of weakness.

It's a no-brainer. If someone's mom or child is sick, or whatever, who even thinks about work? If there's an urgent deadline, someone else on the team can pick it up. Maybe even I'll pick it up. There's support throughout the team and the broader company to say, "OK, go be with your mom, your dad, your kid, and we'll figure out how to get all this done."

The funny thing is, I once had a CEO who was a real hard-ass. He was the kind of guy who managed through fear. But when Tess had the original surgery to reconnect her stomach, he let me go be with my family at the hospital. Maybe he figured there was no point in trying to stop me because I'd be too distracted to work. Or maybe he knew the work wouldn't suffer. Or maybe he was just a father too, so he understood.

That's all empathy is. It's understanding how other people are feeling. You don't have to know the details. You don't have to be overly solicitous. You just have to accept that other people's feelings are different from your own—and as valid as your own. Just because a project or goal at work is the most important thing in your life, that doesn't mean that it's the most important thing in other people's lives.

That's not always easy to remember.

Going Above and Beyond

When we're in the office, I expect work to come first. I don't think anyone should have a problem with that. Tasks need to be done, and they need to be done within a certain time frame. I've never been an advocate for some kind of "Whenever you're ready" approach to deadlines. But a deadline is just a date. It's not something to whip people with. It's not something you should ask people to put before their family's welfare or their own.

Ebbo™ is funded by growth investment, so we need to keep increasing our income to keep our investors happy. The Board of Directors holds us to account. That's their job. Boards can be unforgiving, but they're not inhuman. When your child has to go into surgery Sunday night, most boards don't expect even their CEO to be at work Monday morning—and our board is no different. Part of that was them knowing we consistently execute and deliver as a company. And also knowing that I wouldn't be that effective if I was trying to work in a hospital room when Tess was recovering from surgery.

People will go above and beyond if they know you're supportive of them with whatever life rolls you're dealing with. They in turn will pick up their employee if an employee is in crisis. The team helps each other.

COVID was a great example. Suddenly in spring 2020 everyone was working from home and homeschooling. That's fine if you had teenagers, like I did. At that age people are pretty self-sustaining. But I soon picked up on messages from other folks with younger kids or who didn't have kids. It was more difficult for them. Everyone else picked up on it, too, because without me doing anything about it, people started working around other people's lifestyles.

You send someone a query at 10 a.m. and you might not hear from her all day. Maybe she's busy being the teacher at home for her three kids. Then at 7 or 8 p.m., after bedtime, boom, you get your answer.

Everyone started to appreciate and work around each other's priorities and patterns. That led to a more holistic approach across the board to how we got work done that was different from being in the office. Everyone had a little bit more patience, a little bit more understanding of others.

Everyone had more empathy for everyone else.

It was as if COVID was the biggest team-bonding exercise in history. It was like the whole team was suddenly dropped into a completely unknown wilderness and had to work together to find the way out.

If you're doing your job as a CEO or as a leader, this kind of thing happens instinctively because you've put together a team that doesn't need to be told to be empathetic to others. If you've got that part right, the rest of it follows.

Being a CEO in good times isn't that difficult. Being a CEO when someone's life is falling apart—or when everyone's lives are falling apart, as they did in the pandemic—is far more of a challenge. But it's also when you most need to do your job well. If you support your teams and take care of them, and everyone understands that you do that, the business stuff will fall into line.

Responding to Change

One of my VPs sent me a note one night to say, "This isn't working." She was running a big department, but she had two very young children who had to be fed and occupied during the day. Our old schedules and ways of doing business weren't working. So we postponed some things that we wouldn't normally have put off. And we made it a rule not to schedule calls for lunchtime, when people had to eat or had to feed their kids.

That sort of response to changing circumstances is more than just courtesy. It's a crucial part of getting things done while respecting your team. Empathy demanded that with the new reality of COVID, our business practices had to change to reflect that reality.

You have to set up a culture in which people feel free to bring up issues. And when those issues are brought up, the team or the manager must step in and ask how they can respond. "What can I do?" is an important question for everyone to ask when a team member is having difficulty in their lives. At ebbo™ that aspect of empathy is part of every team member's way of working, including mine.

If there's an important deadline that has to be met and there's no one else to do it, then I will step in and pick up the work and get things done.

Before I joined ebbo™, when I was out of my office for my daughter's recovery from surgery, the rest of the team picked up what I couldn't get done. That experience helped shape my vision for the business. I wanted to create an organization in which a dire life situation did not mean that someone's job or standing in the company was in jeopardy. I wanted a place in which the team worked together and helped each other.

We Have to Talk about This

No business exists in a vacuum. All of us are a part of society and what happens in society affects all of us in business.

A lot of people, however, don't want to talk about the big things that are happening in society. They want to do their work, draw their paychecks, spend time with their families, and that's it. I'm not going to say there's anything wrong with that. I was brought up to not talk about subjects like religion, race, or politics, and I know a lot of people were brought up in the same way. Those topics traditionally polarize views and lead to heated arguments, hurt feelings, and anger and resentment. Who wants that in their lives? Who wants it in their workplace?

Sometimes, though, events outside the business are too large and important to ignore when you get to the office. A good example of that is the murder of George Floyd. The whole country—indeed, the whole world—saw that video of him having his life extinguished by a police officer with a knee on his neck. It was horrific.

It was horrific, but it also wasn't really connected with the company. I felt upset and shocked, like most other Americans, and I discussed it with my family, but in the office I kept my views to myself. Quite soon after the murder, however, some of my team came and asked me what the company's stance was on the incident.

At the time, CEOs from many different companies were making public statements about the murder. They acknowledged that what happened was horrible and unacceptable. They let the world know they were sensitive to the plight of people who have been harmed. I didn't disagree that we should recognize the realities of life: that some groups of citizens in our society have a far worse time than others. But I didn't want to do that. The problem, for me, was that there was never any follow-through.

What did the CEOs in those companies do after their public beating of their breasts and wringing of their hands? Nothing that I could see.

I wanted something different for the company. If I was going to make a statement, I wanted us to take the issues highlighted by George Floyd's murder and confront them as a way to help us grow as individuals and as a business.

I didn't do anything for two weeks, although team members kept coming to me and HR asking us to say something as a company. They were eager that we make some kind of public stand. Finally, after two weeks had passed and I had had some time to consider the situation, I made a video for the team in which I acknowledged the horror and injustice of what happened.

I said I thought the event was going to change us, because it was going to change everybody. I also said that, however anyone chose to think about what had happened, it was important to listen to each other, to understand each other's point of view, and to learn from each other.

I was advocating for empathy at a time when it seemed in short supply in some parts of society. I wanted to start a dialogue.

One thing I did to help the conversation along was to ask one of our VPs, an African American, to share his experiences of living as a Black man in America. At one of our town halls he talked about walking to school one day and being thrown up against a cop car even though he wasn't doing anything wrong. It was harrowing and raw. It opened the eyes of a lot of people on our team. It opened my eyes, too.

I followed up by bringing in a consulting company that works with firms to identify hidden and not-so-hidden bias in hiring, day-to-day operations, and one-on-one interactions. It's not a one-time thing. I want to do a similar exercise every year.

That's the whole point. Justice doesn't come from a single video acknowledging injustice, and empathy doesn't come from one statement by the CEO. Empathy comes from sustained conversation and engagement with issues that affect everyone, and especially minority groups.

Working from the reports that the consultants gave us, we now have a more diverse team and, I believe, a team with more empathy toward one another. We understand each other better and we're more able to treat each other with respect and care.

The actions I took weren't the most significant outcome of the fallout from George Floyd's death, however. Without me, team members created a Diversity Equity Initiative (DEI) within the company. They came to me to ask if they could create an Employee Resource Group to raise awareness of social justice issues within the company—and to do something about them.

It wasn't my idea, and I'm not part of the ERG, but I love that it's there and I love taking part in its events. And I love that they felt that the general culture of tolerance and empathy within the company meant they could approach me with their idea.

The ERG has broadened its purview. It has moved beyond issues of race to look at the challenges faced by women in the workplace, and the particular issues of team members who are parents of autistic children, just to name a few. Every report it issues, every meeting it calls, and every town hall it addresses makes the company a better, more inclusive environment for everyone.

The Power of Youth

No one lives or works in a vacuum. I can't pretend that I came to my newfound sensitivity to diversity issues all by myself.

Like a lot of Americans of my generation, I imagine, I have to give credit to my teenage children.

Young people today know a lot more than we did when we were their age. Or at least more than I did. The internet has made all kinds of experiences and knowledge available to them that simply weren't available back in the day. Some of it is false and dangerous, to be sure, and a lot of it is mindless entertainment, but the overall effect of all this information has got to be a very positive thing.

People form opinions at a younger age because they have more information to base their opinions on. If they want to find out what young Black kids go through, they can watch videos made by those kids about their own experiences. When I listen to my children, I am amazed at what they know and what they have thought about.

That's part of empathy, too. Listening to people that maybe you wouldn't have thought of listening to for wisdom, like my children, taking time to learn about the experiences of others. Like I learned to listen to my kids.

Being a father of socially conscious teenagers has made me think about leadership differently. Like the young people in our two companies, they have a more ideological view of the world and of business than older generations.

They want to have a positive impact. They want to change the world.

Every generation thinks that when they're young, sure, but this seems different to me. These young people don't just imagine change for the better, they articulate it. They come to me to tell me what they'd like the company to do about it.

I'm not necessarily going to implement everything they

want, but I do like the fact that they feel empowered to present issues and ideas so we can evolve and change.

They know I'm always ready to listen.

Clarus Cares

Any company that achieves some success and becomes a little more secure has a certain amount of power in a community. And I believe that power brings responsibility.

You've created a team that can get things done, that can hit deadlines and come up with new ideas. You don't have to restrict all that energy and ability to the bottom line. You can expand beyond your own business and apply that power to the society around you.

Years ago, my aunt and godmother died from cancer. It was devastating and I felt that I had to respond in order to honor her memory. I organized fundraisers for the American Cancer Society for four or five years where I would make a speech about cancer and have a slideshow in tribute to my aunt.

Those events moved people, and it was clear that many of them wanted to help. When I moved to Clarus I decided to expand on that kind of charity work.

I introduced a program called Clarus Cares. It's a vehicle for anyone in the company to join in charitable events. It's not compulsory, but it's very popular. We get about 80 percent participation, so we move things around to give everyone a chance to take time out of the office to contribute. We try to do an external event in the community every quarter. We've worked with Habitat for Humanity and built houses for low-income people. We've done coat drives, shoe drives, and book drives.

During the holiday season we buy gifts for kids from underprivileged homes. We bought items for the veterans' hospital down the street when they were not able to get necessities like soap and shampoo.

When people work together on a charitable project, it increases the ties between them. When you're side by side laying flooring in a house for Habitat for Humanity, you really get to know that person a little better than you might in an office setting.

That's why this charity work doesn't only radiate outward. It has benefits inside the organization, too. It's compassionate, sure, and it helps others, but it also makes us a better, more understanding team.

Being Involved

Many CEOs find it too easy to overlook empathy. It's a little too abstract a quality for them to be comfortable with. It's not easy to quantify. There's no metric for it on a balance sheet.

It never featured high on my priorities until my own brush with death and that of the twins.

Empathy, at its most basic, simply means being open to others and to other influences. It means allowing yourself to get involved with things a business leader might not have considered. The George Floyd tragedy might not seem to have an immediate connection with our business in Connecticut, but we're part of a community and a society—a nation—that was profoundly impacted by the event. It's only human to get involved, and the steps we took have allowed people of diverse backgrounds and abilities to feel like they are supported by management and that they truly are a team.

If people don't back each other up and have each other's backs, they're a team in name only.

You get more effort and better results from people when they feel supported not just by the leadership but by everyone in the team.

The same is true if team members feel they're enabled to think for themselves. Few people are at their best if they just focus on the task in front of them. It's better if they feel able to raise their heads and look at the bigger picture.

It's better if they can think like a CEO.

CHAPTER 4

THINK LIKE A CEO

I t's easy to think like a CEO.

Of course, that's not the same thing as saying it's easy to *be* a CEO. That can be pretty tough at times. And if it's not, it's probably about to be.

But thinking like a CEO really is easy. You just have to be pissed off or frustrated or dissatisfied with what's around you, or to anticipate a problem coming down the track—and come up with the fix.

You just have to lift your head up and look around. It's something I think everyone should be encouraged to do.

Take Mike, my executive vice president. I've known him for a while because we worked together at another firm before we both ended up at ebbo™.

One day when he was still a VP, Mike came to me with an idea to change our loyalty programs. We'd create a range of multiple programs and benefits that would allow us to offer the right program to the right customer, based on their spending patterns. That could increase the likelihood of a customer joining the program because the benefits were more likely to appeal to their specific interests.

The possibilities were endless. In Mike's vision, we'd tailor the programs to each client so they could make sure the array of benefits matched their customers.

The idea had a lot going for it. For one thing, we'd be selling it to folks we were already working with, so we didn't have to go to the work of finding new clients. They already liked us and were happy with what we were doing, so it was a natural step to take.

Mike's idea practically created a new product for us—from something that already existed, but with enough of a twist that it felt like we were offering something new. We didn't even have to do a lot of R&D work. We just pitched it to some clients and ran pilot programs for them. The pilots were a success, and we rolled the program out.

Today it accounts for at least $100 million of our annual business.

And it wouldn't have happened if Mike had been content to simply go along with what we already had. That was fine. Our product was solid. It wasn't just keeping us in business; it was helping us to grow.

That wasn't enough for Mike. He looked at what we had and tried to figure out ways to expand and improve. He was looking at the future, thinking strategically, reaching for innovation.

He was thinking like a CEO.

What Is a CEO?

On the one hand, a CEO is just another team member. That's why I sit with everyone else in our open floor plan. On the other hand, it doesn't really matter where my desk is. It's still the desk where the final decisions get made. The buck stops with me.

Any buck, any time.

That's fine. I was hired to steer the ship, and I'm rewarded well for the pressure and responsibility that comes with it. It's my job to know what course we're on, how the engines are running, whether we need to change the crew or modernize the ship, what the weather conditions are—and where we're sailing next.

I see a CEO as being less a title than a skillset. It's not exclusive. A CEO isn't part of a secret society or an exclusive club.

If people have that skillset, or if you can encourage them to develop it, they can use it whatever their role.

It benefits the whole organization if you encourage others to think like a CEO.

Or, in this case, like Mike.

Don't Stand Alone

Not everyone will want to think like a CEO, even if they can. Some will be content to do their own job without becoming distracted by the larger picture. Their personality is to keep their heads down, work hard to hit deadlines—and then go home and switch off from thinking about what's coming next.

Let them be. They're pure gold—and no business can run without them.

On the other hand, some people will be eager to take the next step in their career. If they're like me before my operation, they may well be a little *too* eager. There's a difference, however, between being too ambitious to get a new title and wanting to change the level at which you think and act.

Anyone in an organization can think and act strategically and innovatively. If they do that, their reward in terms of title and money will come. The key is to start thinking like a CEO *before* you're being paid to be one.

Encourage people to think that way because it makes their job more interesting and them more effective. Encourage them because it benefits the whole team and supports you as the CEO. Encourage them because one day you'll need to hire a new CEO to sit where you sit now.

Thinking Strategically

When my daughters were fighting to stay alive, neither my wife nor I had any energy to think about anything other than getting through the next few minutes or the next few hours.

Thinking in terms of whole days was an unimaginable luxury.

Fortunately, we were surrounded by health professionals whose job was to think further ahead, to the mid- or long term. They had to take a strategic view: how best could we get to our goal of two healthy, happy babies?

Even Dr. Death was looking ahead, although in his case the future was gray and bleak.

Businesses face emergencies all the time. It goes without saying that they are not literal matters of life or death, like a medical emergency, but that doesn't mean they're not serious in their own way for the people involved. A short deadline, a delayed report, an absent colleague, an angry client: when you're in the middle of crises, they can overwhelm you.

You get dragged into the day-to-day. Firefighting, blocking and tackling, plate spinning, crisis management. Whatever you call it, it's not what the CEO should be doing.

At least, not all the time.

If the CEO is down in the weeds with the team, the business can never grow.

A successful business needs to project years, not days or weeks or even months. As CEO you have to get off the phone, get out of meetings, pick your head up from your desk, and think strategically.

You need to look at the next quarter, the next year, even the next decade.

It's not just what you're doing now. It's what you could be doing now. And what you'll be doing in the future, or what you could be doing. And how you get there.

It's not thinking about what time the twins next need to be fed. It's thinking way into the future about the times when one needs a ride to the ballpark and the other needs a ride to the cinema.

Innovation Attitude

If someone brings an idea to me, the first thing I do is try to destroy it.

I have them write it up on a whiteboard and then start to pick holes in it. I look for weaknesses. I look for fail points. I look for miscalculations of costs. I ask a ton of questions, and each one is a hurdle where the idea can fall.

I hate to do it. Before anything even reaches my desk, someone has thought hard about it and put in a lot of work. But those things aren't enough.

The team knows I'll stress-test something to destruction if I can. It's how we avoid wasting time.

But that's exactly the reason most people fear bringing an idea forward: in case it fails.

That's human nature.

But you can't innovate without failure. You can't be a consistent.300 hitter without first hitting a lot of foul balls and striking out. You have to put in the time and effort to learn how to hit, and that means you will fail at hitting a lot before you get good.

Hell, even when you *are* a.300 hitter, which means you're a sensational batter, you are still failing to get a hit 70 percent of the time.

My job is not to stop people from failing. It's to make sure that they don't mind failing. It's to make sure that their failure doesn't stop them in their tracks but spurs them on.

It reminds me of the famous quote from the Irish writer Samuel Beckett. "Ever tried. Ever Failed. No Matter. Try Again. Fail Again. Fail Better."

I'm aware of the contradiction. I encourage people to innovate and bring me new ideas—and then I put a lot of energy into throwing ideas out.

The team knows why I'm doing it. It's not because I'm not open to new ideas. It's the very opposite. There are so many ideas that we need to be sure which ones deserve to have money and time sunk into them.

A lot of ideas die on my desk. I tell everyone that that's not failure. A true failure doesn't teach you anything. From all our failures, we learn. And we keep trying to innovate. We keep taking chances—and no one pays the price if they don't come off.

Because once in a while, a Mike is going to smash it out of the park.

House Key

I was a Mike once. Years ago, when I was still a junior exec at a different company, I learned that CEO-think can come from anywhere.

For me, innovation came in the aisles at Home Depot.

I'd just sunk all of my savings into buying my first condo, but it needed some fixing up. I couldn't afford to pay anyone, so I learned to do it myself. I read up about maintenance, I bought tools and supplies, and I did the work myself.

In the late 1990s, the home improvement movement was just taking off. Stores like Home Depot and Lowe's were appearing everywhere, and every time I went to the store, I saw lots of other people doing *exactly the same thing as me*.

They were a completely new yet clearly defined market: homeowners doing their own home repairs.

I went home and spent the weekend with a legal pad figuring out how our company could serve the new market.

I thought like a CEO. I came up with what I called House Key, a program that gave DIYers a discount at Home Depot or Lowe's. I described it as "unlocking the savings in your home." I wrote my own business plan.

On Monday I brought the idea to my boss. I'd worked hard, so I was ready to answer the hailstorm of questions I knew she was going to throw at me. Then she called in the rest of the team to brainstorm the idea, so that it got stretched and pulled this way and that.

Not only did it survive, it went live and became a great revenue generator for the company.

Not bad for an idea that struck in a shopping aisle.

Thinking like a CEO is being alert to the sort of opportunities that connect the world around you to your business. You learn to take the kind of idle thought other people let cross their minds and disappear, and you hold on to it and examine what it means. You ask "What if?" and "What if?" again. You learn to cultivate curiosity about what's happening in the world—because sooner or later that's what's going to shape your market.

Anyone who thinks like a CEO should be keeping track of whatever is interesting or different in any area of life. They should want to be the best-informed person in the company.

If you're not, work at it harder!

Kitchen Table Economics

On the bottom line, every business decision is a financial decision. Landing a new client, hiring more people, expanding into another city, renovating the office, changing employment contracts: everything a CEO signs off on is judged, sooner or later, by how it impacts the balance sheet.

That impact might not always be direct. It might seem completely unrelated. But everything factors into the financial wellness of the business.

One of the first things I did when the doctors told me I had to have open-heart surgery was to run more and hit the gym. It seems unrelated—even counterintuitive—but it seemed to me that the fitter I got before the surgery, the quicker my recovery would be. It impacted the bottom line.

Corporate finance is often highly complex. That's why every business has CFOs, accountants, bookkeepers, etc. Some CEOs love to get into the detail—and every CEO has to *know* the detail—but I find it helps to make top-down decisions by simply stripping away the office and my colleagues and putting myself back at the kitchen table at home.

That's where my wife, Michelle, and I look over our bills. That's where we check our bank balance and talk about what's coming up: trips to take the girls to see colleges, maybe a family vacation, some landscaping work in the yard. We look at how much money we have, how much we need, and how to allocate it.

Like virtually every other family in the country.

I'm not pretending it's a revolutionary process. It's common sense, simple math—and an understanding that you can't necessarily have everything you want.

You have to prioritize.

It's exactly the same in business. Approach a decision the same way you would approach it at your kitchen table. And using your own money.

That last phrase is key.

It's tempting to imagine thinking like a CEO involves nothing but front-of-plane seats, five-star hotels, and fancy restaurants. It's how big shots behave. And it's all on the company anyway.

If it's not clear by now, I don't go for that idea of the CEO. And the company's money is just as real as your family's money. Thinking like a CEO isn't coming up with ways to take advantage of that. It's coming up with ways to use it for the best investment for the business. If you're working straight after you get off the airplane and you need to be fresh, sure, fly club. If not, save the money.

Imagine you're sitting at your kitchen table. If it would be a self-indulgent extravagance there, it probably is in the office, too.

Be thoughtful. Respect the business. Respect the money. Invest it accordingly.

If a team member comes to me with an idea to do some testing on a potential product, the cost of the testing doesn't matter. What is important is the cost of the test compared with the possible benefit it will bring. We can spend hundreds of thousands of dollars to test a new product—but only if that new product has a realistic likelihood of earning millions.

Hard Conversations

It sounds like heresy in business, but the customer is not always right.

In any client-driven business, the CEO has to recognize the times when the interests of your company and the interests of your clients don't line up.

It's not easy. You want to please your clients. It's your *job* to please your clients. But there are times when you have to say no. There are times they want something too quickly or too cheaply, or too technically difficult. Sometimes they want resources that are allocated elsewhere.

Sometimes, they take advantage of your relationship to ask for more than they're paying for.

It's tough. But the CEO's job is to be in those tough situations, make tough conversations—and back them up with tough calls with the client.

Your foremost job is to protect your company, just as much as pleasing clients and lining up future business.

So maybe you have to tell a client that you can't do what they want in a particular case. If you've had a good relationship in the past, and if you've laid the groundwork of good communication and mutual understanding, maybe it will go well. On the other hand, sometimes the client will push back. They might get nasty, or scream and yell.

Big-head CEOs don't like being told no.

It's your job to massage the message and present it the best you can: not with a punch but in a velvet glove.

It's something all leaders should be empowered and willing to do: to realize that the interests of the business come first, even at the risk of short-term pain and client displeasure.

But remember that if there's a serious client rift, there's only one person in the organization who will have to step in!

Rewards

Being a CEO has a lot of rewards. Remuneration is just part of it. Once you have a certain level of lifestyle, that doesn't matter so much. What matters is seeing your company prosper and become financially stable. Or successfully selling it to open the next chapter of its history.

What motivates me more than anything else is seeing talented people grow by helping them gain skills, gain promotions, and take on new responsibilities. When someone moves up from a coordinator to become a VP or even to go run another company, it's as exciting to me as if I were doing it myself.

I *want* people to succeed. I believe any good CEO wants the same thing, because it proves that they've got the right people around them. The more those people can think like a CEO—the more they innovate and strategize to improve the bottom line on behalf of the company—the more they support the CEO and the more they benefit the whole company.

That's how you face the future. That's how you get past the Dr. Deaths prophesying doom. That's how you have a whole team trying to anticipate what's over the horizon—and looking forward to it.

Things will go wrong, of course. But you'll be future proofed. And in any case, it's not good to get too comfortable. You miss what's going on around you.

Being uncomfortable is part of being a CEO. It can engender a state of mind where it becomes a source of power and energy for you. In the next chapter we'll see how that works.

CHAPTER 5

GET COMFORTABLE WITH THE UNCOMFORTABLE

Going under the knife for open-heart surgery is a pro-foundly uncomfortable experience. It's not just being in the hospital and having your life turned upside down. There is the disorientation coming out of anesthesia, the pain from the procedure, the lack of privacy that comes with being in the hospital—and the nagging worry that you might not survive the procedure.

What was most uncomfortable by far was that I had no control over what was happening to me. The trajectory I had thought my life was on had been derailed. The future I thought that I was responsible for creating for myself now lay entirely in the hands of others. Going into the OR was a leap of faith for someone like me who naturally wants to be in control. You put your body in the care of a team of professionals and trust they'll do their jobs right to fix what's wrong with you and to keep you alive while they're doing it.

I couldn't control the medical procedure at all, especially once I was under. So I reacted by concentrating on the things that I could control. In this case, I got myself in the best shape possible before the surgery by working out and building up my stamina. And as soon as I could after surgery, the next day, I made sure to get out of bed and start walking.

I couldn't control the surgery, but I could control the rehab.

It was the same story when the twins were born prematurely. No one could control when my wife went into labor ten weeks early. And after the girls were born, we had to rely entirely on others for getting them through.

That wasn't just uncomfortable. It was terrifying.

Those two brushes with critical medical care taught me a lot. They taught me that discomfort is unavoidable—but that you can learn to live with it. And they taught me that, if you learn to be comfortable with discomfort, you can turn it into a positive.

After my open-heart surgery, I was back in the office less than a month later because I'd taken control of my rehab. After the girls' births, we organized a family rotation to care for them that helped get them home as soon as possible.

I didn't die. The girls grew up healthy.

Both times, we got through the discomfort.

Seizing Control

My most recent source of discomfort has been on a completely different level, as it has for everyone in the world. When COVID hit in 2020, it wasn't just out of my control. It was out of everyone's control.

It was nature in overdrive.

No one knew how the virus would spread. No one knew when the vaccine was going to be ready. No one knew who in our team might get sick. No one knew how working at home would affect business. No one even knew what the business would look like when we came out the other side.

There were so many questions and so few answers. Or rather, so many answers...but with no guarantee any of them were right.

Like millions of CEOs around the world, I still had to run a business at the same time as ensuring the safety of my loved ones.

I controlled what I could—and learned to be comfortable with what I couldn't.

We couldn't alleviate the pandemic, but we set out to help the team deal with it as well as they could. We worked more flexibly. By the time Christmas came, we gave everyone two weeks off so they could get some relief from the mental fatigue that came from working at home, having sick relatives, home-schooling, and whatever.

The other lesson I brought from medicine to the CEO's desk was not to try to control things I knew little about. I trusted the experts. On the one hand, that meant trusting that the authorities, the CDC, and the medical researchers would give the best advice and do their jobs to the best of their ability. On the other hand, it also meant trusting my team.

It was the head of HR who was put on the spot when the pandemic hit. It was her job to work through remote ways of working. They weren't procedures I could control to any meaningful degree. When she recommended a course of action, I went with her expertise.

There's no roadmap for emergency surgery. There is no MBA class in how to react to events like the pandemic or 9/11.

Any leader has to figure it all out as he or she goes along. It's not going to be easy and it's not going to be comfortable.

And you need to be comfortable with that.

Death, Taxes, and Discomfort

Discomfort will always be with you. It's a constant for any leader. As a CEO you can't wait to act until a situation is sorted out, calmed down, or comfortable. That is not going to happen. One of the main reasons you're in the CEO's seat is to be able to find order in chaos.

During chaotic times your business doesn't stand still. There are deadlines to hit, board meetings to attend, clients to please, targets to meet. None of those are put on hold while you get comfortable with whatever situation you are in.

In a crisis, your team will look to you for direction and a sense of normalcy. Those are the minimum requirements to keep your organization running well. They'll also help your team feel a whole lot better—and everyone else they interact with, too.

At ebbo™, I have 260-plus team members, which is a lot of folks depending on my judgment. And it's not only them but their partners and kids and anyone who relies on their income and their mental and emotional well-being.

If I make a bad decision, the ripple effect can affect thousands of people.

That realization can be a source of real discomfort—but it's crucial for CEOs to be able to think like this.

Preparation Removes Fear

Not being comfortable with discomfort undermines your ability to make decisions. It can bring on fear of making a decision in case you make a mistake—and that's a seriously bad outcome, because as CEO your job description is practically nothing *but* making decisions. You have to be in a good mental state to make the tough calls.

Hell, you have to be in a good mental state to make the *easy* calls.

I tell my family and my team members all the time: preparation removes fear. In fact, I say it so much that it's often met with a lot of eye rolls. It might sound like a cliché from any sports locker room, but that doesn't stop it from being true.

Most of us learned this lesson in school. If you go into an exam unprepared, you will usually be plagued with fear. On the other hand, if you spend the necessary time beforehand applying yourself to the material and doing everything you can to absorb the knowledge you need, you're a whole lot more confident because you've gone a long way toward ensuring your success.

It's no different in business. If you're going into a meeting, you should know everything about the issue at hand. If you're pitching a potential new client, you should know them thoroughly to predict their needs. You should know your presentation inside and out, so you have a strong answer if you are challenged on any aspect of it.

Practice all the questions you could get at a meeting. Practice answering every question you can think of—and then get a colleague or your spouse to think of the questions you didn't even think of...and practice answering them, too.

You not only prepare, you *over*prepare. Leave nothing to chance. Make sure the answers become second nature.

Preparation trumps fear. Every time. It is the best way to bring some degree of comfort into the constant discomfort that business throws at you.

Catastrophic Thinking Is Counterproductive

It's easy to fall into catastrophic thinking when a crisis hits. When the girls were going through their difficulties in those early months, I could have fallen down any number of rabbit holes imagining the worst outcomes of their surgeries or the limited lives they might have to lead in the future.

That kind of apocalyptic approach is frighteningly easy to fall into. Many of us naturally see how things can go wrong and follow that train of thought all the way to disaster.

But thinking like that wouldn't have helped me or my wife—and it certainly wouldn't have helped the girls.

Changing that attitude is a question of changing your mindset. It's not easy but it's possible. Preparation and trying to see other ways things can turn out are ways out of catastrophic thinking.

The twins are all grown up now, and one of them got a job while she was in high school that sometimes required her to work more hours than she wanted. One time, a change in rotation or covering for an absence meant that she was asked to work a ten-hour shift two days in a row.

This was not to her liking, to put it mildly.

I listened to her complain and I asked her to reframe how she was looking at it. She was seeing it exclusively as a bad thing, an imposition that took away her free time. I encouraged her to think about it from another point of view. She would get through her two shifts, and on the other side she'd have all this money that she didn't have before and wasn't expecting. That's a far more positive outcome.

She couldn't control her employer's schedule, but she could control how she reacted to it. She could look to the benefits rather than the downside.

It worked. Once she started thinking about the extra cash, she felt a lot better about her schedule.

Meanwhile, her twin sister is an avid reader and wanted to get a job at the local bookstore, but she was afraid to go in and ask for an application. I'm not sure if she thought it would be embarrassing, but it became a big issue in her mind.

One day when we were driving by the bookstore, I stopped and told her she was going in and asking for an application. Her fears meant that she didn't want to, but I insisted. Eventually she went in and came out with an application, and I could see on her face she was happy about it.

The experience had been a lot easier than she thought. She

changed her attitude, ditched the catastrophic thinking, and just figured out the steps she needed to take to get her father off her back. So she conquered her fear. She filled out the application and got the job—and she loves it!

In any situation that has fear attached to it, it's important to figure out what you can control and take control of those elements. Whatever level of control you have in a situation, which may be very little, get comfortable with it and use it to do whatever you can. Then move on.

Don't Be a Victim

I've always felt that my heart surgery gave me a second chance—and one I didn't even know I needed. The scar on my chest reminded me every day that I had dodged a bullet. I hadn't even heard the shot.

That second chance reminded me that living life is more important than doing well in business. Family is more important than doing well in business. And yet business is also really important. It still means a lot to me. But it doesn't define me now in the way I think it sometimes defined Tom 1.0.

My daughters, of course, don't remember the traumatizing times they went through as babies. My wife and I certainly do. So do the rest of the family who were around at the time. The girls' lack of awareness of that despair is both a blessing and a curse. It's a blessing because I wouldn't want them to remember an experience that was so distressing. And it's a curse because I sometimes think that having those memories would help them appreciate their lives more.

It would put everything in perspective, just like my surgery did for me.

They would understand that working long shifts or having to walk up to a stranger and ask for a job application are not big deals. Not in the grand scheme of things—and not in the stories of their lives.

I'd never belittle other people's problems, and I understand that something that might seem trivial to me could be a big deal to someone else. But a lot of the problems we let dominate our lives, especially at work, are not life-and-death issues. They're not even close.

That doesn't mean they're not serious, but it means they're surmountable.

When you've had a taste of actual life-and-death issues, that perspective becomes remarkably clear.

I like to think that I've always had this attitude, but I suspect that my empathy comes from my brushes with serious illness. That's why I think I'm a far better CEO than my younger self ever could have been. And a much better person.

Sometimes when I see young families expecting a baby, the parents often talk a lot about whether they'd prefer a boy or a girl. Having been through what we went through, it's an irrelevant question. The only thing that matters is that the baby is healthy.

That might not seem particularly profound as an observation, but it comes from great suffering. You don't have to go through the same kind of trauma I did to come to such realizations.

I learned a lot from what happened—but thankfully not everyone has to go through the same experience to learn the same lessons.

What's around the Next Corner?

None of us has to be a victim of circumstance when our lives or businesses are thrown out of kilter. There are always places in the chaos where we can take some control and relieve some of the discomfort. It's not always easy to find those places, but they are there. It's a question of figuring out what you can change, what you have to accept, and what you can work around.

A CEO needs to go through this process constantly. It's a constant process of assessment, action, and letting go, which is why flexibility and curiosity is a far more useful mindset than dogmatism and certainty. As a CEO, you need to think about what's coming—even when *no one* knows what's coming, like at the start of the pandemic.

You need to look not only at what's in front of you, but at what's around the corner or even away over the horizon, because that unknown lurking out of sight could be a game changer for your business, your life, or the world.

Could anyone have anticipated the Great Resignation, the upheaval in the job market that came in the wake of the pandemic? A smart CEO could. Perhaps not in any detail, or with a precise appreciation of its scale, but a CEO on top of current events would have the tools to have at least anticipated it as a possibility.

Once people figured out they could work from home, it's not a big leap to anticipate that a certain number of people would want to always work from home. Some workers would have no interest in making a daily commute if they don't have to be in a particular building to do their work.

From that understanding, it's inevitable that New York companies might start casting their net wide to recruit talent with that perk in mind. They can offer a big-city salary while their people live in small-town America and don't have to pay New York prices for housing and transportation. That's very attractive to a lot of people. It's a game changer for the job market.

And it was entirely predictable for a CEO who took it upon him- or herself to ask the question, to consider the future, to look around the corner.

The task now for CEOs is to anticipate what it will mean. Will real estate prices take a dive? Will some cities become ghost towns? Will we lose our smartest people to big-city employers? Those are the questions that gnaw away at business leaders as they consider how to lead out of the pandemic.

Our team members all worked remotely from early in the pandemic. The office was shuttered for well over a year. Yet I actually believe that having a team sharing a physical location has definite advantages. It creates a more cohesive and cooperative community. It offers benefits from interaction and in-person collaboration.

I wanted to get people back. But the reality is that if I mandated compulsory attendance, I would lose team members. I had to accept that some people wanted to work from home now.

None of this was easy. It took work and flexibility. I wasn't comfortable with it—and yet I had to accept it.

Accept what you can't change and work to change what you can to your advantage.

That's what business is: getting things done when getting things done is uncomfortable.

Change Happens

Running any business is not a simple thing. The pandemic reminded us of that, but even without the pandemic the sheer number of variables and uncertainties can be overwhelming.

Technologies change constantly, and work culture changes too. Some team members want flexible hours and the ability to work at home; others prefer to come to the office. Even your core business can change.

Change can come out of nowhere...and it can come fast. Imagining its consequences can be a huge source of discomfort. But while the pandemic was a singular event—one hopes— change is a constant. It's a process and it's the natural environment in which any CEO has to operate.

Change is often uncomfortable, but that doesn't mean it's not surmountable. It's most rewarding when you embrace it and, as we'll see in the next chapter, it's easiest to embrace when you're prepared for it.

CHAPTER 6

STAY HUMBLE,
STAY HUNGRY

In my teens, I was crazy for sports, especially baseball and golf. I wasn't always the best player on the team, but I was almost always the captain. That was because I was the best leader.

Back then, I didn't think being a leader required any humility. I was super confident. I felt like I was indestructible. Whatever I tackled, I knew I would do well. I took that sense of confidence into my adulthood and just ran with it. My sense of being indestructible propelled me through life. It gave me the skills, knowledge, and confidence to move up in the business world.

I couldn't understand people who were not leaders or who were not driven. They were a mystery to me. I did not see how different personalities approached life in different ways. I thought only my way was valid.

Then, of course, I learned in no uncertain terms that my sense of being indestructible was a complete illusion.

A trip to the OR destroyed that fantasy.

But that brush with death reminded me that when I played all those sports, I wasn't just learning about leadership. I also learned about teamwork.

I wasn't too aware of that at the time, but the reset after my surgery made the lesson far clearer. I can barely think of any decision I've made in business that wasn't a collaborative effort.

A CEO never plays the game alone.

What I realized was that the world was bigger than just me. I couldn't always score the goal, make the tackle, or pick up the rebound. I had to rely on others. I didn't always have to be *the* guy.

It's always humbling to realize that we have to rely upon others. But it turns out that humility isn't a weakness. It doesn't lower my expectations of myself. It doesn't stop me trying to excel and make my business the best it could be.

Humility is a powerful motivation to stay hungry to improve and learn. It acknowledges that I don't know everything. And that means that I'm not going to get stuck in old modes of thinking or outdated ways of doing business.

Every leader needs a sense of humility. It keeps him or her ready for the next step, whatever that might be.

Marathon Mind

In the middle of a race, most marathon runners look like the most miserable people on the planet. There's pain all over their faces. They're desperate for it to stop.

My father ran marathons. He completed fifteen or so over the course of his running career. As a young adult, I would go watch his races and wonder why he or any of the other runners would put themselves through the agony.

Gradually my attitude changed. So many people got involved in marathons, so many people did them over and again, that I wondered if there was maybe something to it after all. I wondered if I had it in me to run a marathon.

Once that idea took hold, I put a plan together and did the training and preparation I needed to do. And I ran my marathon.

If anything, the marathon made me even more convinced that I could do anything. It made me feel I could run right up to a wall, crash through it, and keep going on the other side.

That was a year or two before the doctors discovered the heart problem that led to the operating table.

It turned out that the training and the race could have killed me. A marathon puts a huge strain on your body. I could have ended up in a very bad place at any time.

I got lucky, but it was a close escape—and another lesson in humility. Charging hard has its benefits, but it also has its downsides. Sometimes a hard-charger lacks the humility to pause and understand him or herself.

The marathon mind can take over and push everything else aside because of a basic lack of humility.

No Room for Complacency

I'm not advocating for the elimination of drive. I'm advocating humility as an asset for any leader—hell, for any individual.

Being humble means not getting too high or too low.

It doesn't mean not celebrating your wins, because celebrations are a necessary part of any successful business. It doesn't mean not being pissed about your losses, because losses are painful. But it does mean keeping a sense of perspective.

Your wins are not the be-all and end-all of your life. There could be a loss around the next corner. And your losses are not causes for despair, because things could improve tomorrow. You're never as awesome or as useless as you feel.

Running a business is a series of ups and downs. You're unlikely to be able to change those ups and downs much, so your task is to help the team to see them for what they are: opportunities to learn, grow, and get better.

It Takes All Kinds

It took learning some humility for me to realize that lots of people were not wired like me.

That would have come as a complete surprise to Tom 1.0.

Years ago, a company I was working at got everyone to take a personality test called Insights Discovery. You work through the questionnaire and then your answers are analyzed and you're given a color based on how they break down.

I was red. That meant I was hard driving. I absorbed information quickly, made quick decisions, and took quick action.

I got on with whatever was at hand.

I thought the most successful business should be full of people like me, who strove for success at the expense of everything else. I thought everyone should be a red. None of the other colors made any sense to me.

My attitude was the one that worked.

I took the same test again twenty years later. I was still a solid red. I was hard-driven. But this time I paid more attention to the other possible colors. I once had a director who took the same Insights Discovery questionnaire. She came out as a blue. That meant she was almost the complete opposite of red. She took things slowly. She needed time to consider information thoroughly and assess the ramifications of various courses of action. She needed to ask questions and think about the answers.

It could hardly be different from my way of doing things. In the past, I would have gotten pissed and impatient. Now I'm more appreciative of different approaches. I still might get impatient sometimes, but now I see the value of bringing different perspectives and approaches into the mix.

I had everyone at ebbo™ take the Insights Discovery test. It was a huge advantage in how we understood each other and handled one-on-one interactions—and that helped us find different ways of working through problems.

Not only are your personality and approach not the only ones. They're not necessarily even the best for a particular situation. Acknowledging that reality is humbling—but it's also the first step in allowing others to be capable and productive in their own way.

Staying Hungry

Some CEOs like to stay within their comfort zone as much as possible. I think that makes you bored and stale. A CEO who stays humble is always hungry to learn and grow. They want to get better. They want to tackle the next big challenge. They lean into tasks they've not done before that are going to take them out of their depth.

When we acquired another company, we increased our size from about 170 team members to 260. That represented a huge change for me as a CEO. Before the acquisition I knew all my team members. I knew their working styles, their strengths, the way they interacted with others, even their family situations.

And they knew me, of course.

After the acquisition I suddenly knew nothing at all about half of my new team. I went from understanding every moving part of the business to not knowing how they all fit together.

It was unsettling, but it was exciting, too, because it was a chance to grow as a CEO.

I had to figure out a way to get to know the new folks as quickly as possible, so I introduced myself at a team meeting. I knew that some of them—maybe a lot of them—were likely suspicious of me. Getting a new boss can be traumatic at the best of times, let alone when his company has just acquired yours.

You feel like your life is in the hands of a stranger you can't even tell if you can trust.

For that reason, I was careful not to stand up and tell them about our rules and culture. I told them about myself: that I was married with three teenage children. That I go to Tess's plays and Grace's volleyball games. That I love baseball and watching my son, Tommy, excel at it.

That was far more important than telling them how I expected them to do things from now on. It was more effective than trying to make out that I was the smartest or the most accomplished person in the room. I doubt I was either, so I didn't even try.

It was more important to tell them that I didn't necessarily know it all. That I was humble enough to learn from them instead of just telling them what to do.

Curiosity Is Key

I was never much of a reader in high school or college. In those days, I was more interested in sports than knowledge. It was only after college that something clicked in my head and I became an active learner.

Now I read books all the time: self-help books, business books, nonfiction, even some novels. It's the only way to ensure that I keep learning. I never know what I might find in one of these books that I can bring back to ebbo™ and help make us better companies.

Learning new things is curiosity in action. It's finding whatever might be coming next that looks most interesting and diving into it to see what it is, how it works, and where it might fit into my life.

I constantly try to push myself physically as well as mentally. I sometimes think of myself as an experiment, always trying new and different things. I love to try strict disciplines regarding food and exercise. I was a vegan for years and ate gluten-free. Then I tried the keto diet.

You learn about these things by doing them.

Like growing a business.

I joined Clarus Commerce as president and COO of a ten-person company. I then became CEO and we grew to 170 people. The step up to nearly 300 people is just the next step.

I'm curious to see how it works out.

Learning from the Board

The humble, hungry CEO can learn from anywhere.

In our regular board meetings, I could go on my own as the face of our day-to-day operations and sit up at the end of the table, where the "leader" usually sits. Instead, I bring in the entire leadership team and deliberately sit in the middle of the table. When all is said and done, we're not there to boost our egos. I know I'm not the smartest person in the room—but I also know I don't have to be.

We're there so that the board and team can ask each other questions and exchange information.

Approached with the right amount of humility, the board meeting is a learning experience for everyone.

When the company made its acquisition, one of our board members was a former CEO of a couple of companies that had bought a dozen or so companies, so he knew a lot of the ins and outs of acquisition. When we were going through the process, I used him as a mentor. He explained the different approaches, and what had worked for him and what had been a disaster.

The acquisition was a new experience for me, so the more I could learn from him the better.

I'd like eventually to join the boards of other companies. That's partly because I think my experience means I'll be able to make a contribution—but it's also partly because it's another opportunity to learn. It's the next stage in being an active learner and seeing how different companies approach problems and challenges in different ways.

Curiosity and the willingness to learn are humility in action. It's letting yourself be ready to acquire new skills and new knowledge. It's the best way to keep yourself and your business strong.

Change Is an Opportunity

Everyone knows that nothing stands still. A process that works for you today might be obsolete tomorrow. You might think you have the best approach to a situation, but a competitor can show you a better way.

You won't learn that better way if you're not curious. If you don't have the humility to realize that you *need* to be curious, all sorts of opportunities will pass you by.

Business leaders either keep learning or they get left behind. If they keep their eyes down as they charge blindly forward, they'll never discover whether there might be a better way.

I went from blind faith in my own ability to a state of humility where I realized that everyone I work with has something to teach me—and that I wanted to learn.

I learned those lessons through medical emergencies that took me into the valley of the shadow of death. I'm writing this book so that you don't need to go through a similar trauma to keep yourself hungry and curious.

That hunger, coupled with preparation, is what sets you up for consistent success.

CHAPTER 7

THERE'S NO SUCH THING AS OVERPREPARATION

When we turned forty, a few of my friends and I decided to celebrate the milestone by taking part in a Tough Mudder, a ten-mile endurance race through several extreme environments.

It was a typical middle-aged decision. We wanted to think of ourselves as being young and healthy.

Tough Mudders are designed to stretch people's physical and mental abilities by placing them in seriously dangerous conditions.

We had six months to get into shape, so I committed to a rigorous fitness routine. I started running regularly. I lifted weights. I ate right. I did everything I could to get my body and mind ready.

When the event came round, I was in good shape. We traveled up to the event, and as we sat around the night before, a couple of the others told me they were nervous. They knew they hadn't prepared enough.

I had no nerves. I was calm and ready to go.

Next day, the race went exactly as you would expect. I got around in pretty good shape, and got a huge buzz from the achievement. The other guys straggled in at the back of the field, cursing the day they had taken on the challenge.

I'd looked at the end goal, I'd put together a training plan, and I'd executed it. I studied the difficulties I would face during the event—but I trained to overcome even greater challenges. On the day, I had no nerves and no doubt. I knew I could do it because I'd overprepared.

It won't surprise anyone to learn that someone who prepares for a physical challenge is going to do better than someone who doesn't.

The same should be equally obvious about business.

Preparation works. And overpreparation works better.

What's Wrong with Being Nervous?

Some people say that being nervous is a benefit. It keeps them alert and sharp for occasions such as big meetings, the same way stage fright keeps actors at their very best.

I didn't use to see it that way. When I was an assistant manager, I wasn't just nervous before a meeting with a client: I was actually scared. That wasn't an enjoyable feeling and it hindered more than it helped. Being so nervous, I couldn't be my authentic self—and someone who is not authentic can't come across as transparent or trustworthy.

Looking back, I realize that I got so nervous because I lacked the experience to know how to prepare. That experience only came thanks to time—and my visits to the hospital.

Today I overprepare because it allows me to be less nervous. If I'm more myself, I relax, and I increase the odds of getting a good outcome from a meeting.

I'm most relaxed without notes or scripts. When speakers use notes to cover up their nervousness, it telegraphs to the audience that the speaker doesn't know their material well enough. That doesn't inspire confidence. And a scripted presentation usually sounds worse than inauthentic; it sounds robotic.

I lose interest and I know everyone else in the room does, too.

I learn my material inside out, so I don't need notes or a script.

Repetition Unlocks Confidence

A while ago I learned the Rocks and Pebbles method in a class on presentations.

You memorize your opening and closing statements. In between, you position three or four "rocks," which are your major themes. The "pebbles" are the talking points that come off those rocks.

If you remember the rocks, you don't have to remember the pebbles. The rocks will trigger your memory so the pebbles come up naturally.

It's great because I don't have to memorize everything. I just get my opening, my closing, and all my rocks lined up, and go through them again and again until they become second nature.

I taught the Rocks and Pebbles method to an assistant manager at ebbo™ who had to give a presentation to the whole team and was very nervous. She memorized her opening and closing, and got the rocks fixed in her mind. She spent weeks rehearsing—and she nailed the presentation.

It doesn't have to be Rocks and Pebbles, but you need a method. It doesn't matter what it is, as long as it works for you. If it's effective, though, I can promise you one thing.

It involves a lot of repetition.

Every year, I give a big speech at our annual holiday dinner. I look at what we've done and where we're going, I celebrate our successes and explain our failures frankly.

I rehearse for weeks ahead of the meeting. If I'm in my car driving, I rehearse the speech. If I'm waiting in a line, I rehearse my speech. If I'm taking a shower, I rehearse my speech. I don't only run through it in my head. Sometimes, I actually say it out loud to myself.

It never comes out the same, but that doesn't matter. If I hit the rocks, I know I can fill in the stones. And that allows me to be as authentic as I can, so the team recognizes me as the same guy they know throughout the rest of the year.

Prepare for the Expected

I'd sold the company three times over the years before we made our acquisition. Each time was a challenge because each time was different.

We couldn't learn from experience.

Before we met with any prospective buyer, we had to know our metrics cold going back over years. We had to explain the present and project the future. Then we had to get up and explain it to twenty or thirty members of their team.

Then it was open season. They got to question us on every detail of the business, no matter how minor. A blip in the financials ten years previously might need as much explanation as something that happened last week. People got sidetracked by the tiniest issues. They thought they saw issues when there were none.

Everyone wanted to show why they were in the meeting. Everyone wanted to demonstrate that they'd done their due diligence.

This went on for hours.

There was no time for research and no room for guesswork. We had to give answers in real time.

So we overprepared. We went through every possible question. We examined the strengths and weaknesses of our history. We learned all we could about the potential buyers: the CEO, the partners, any associate who might be involved.

What were they going to ask us? What was the worst gotcha question they could come up with?

There's always a gotcha question. If you put a bunch of ambitious associates in a meeting where they get a chance to impress their own partners, they all bring their own gotcha question.

They want to prove their smarts.

They were always the people most likely to embarrass us—so we had to make sure we knew the answers.

We knew the questions were coming, so we prepared for them.

As we left one long meeting with potential buyers, my senior vice president said, "I can't believe we answered every question. It was like a shark tank in there."

We succeeded because we overprepared. With over-preparation, there are no shark tanks; there are only dips in the pool.

Prepare for the Unexpected Eventuality

It's one thing to prepare for what you know is coming. It's completely different to prepare for the unexpected. No one knows what's over the horizon.

It might be a potentially fatal heart condition. It might be seriously sick kids.

All you can do is control what you can and keep an eye on the future. Anticipate a day out, a week out, a month out—and then as far out as possible.

Every CEO has to be on top of the day-to-day operations of their business, but no CEO can succeed if that's all they do. Even if no one else in the organization has time or inclination to look ahead, the CEO has to. They can't just think about today or even this year. They have to try to anticipate a year or two ahead. They have to think about three-year goals, even ten-year goals.

A good CEO spends at least some of the time looking over the horizon. What's out there is unknown—but that doesn't mean you can't prepare for it now. The key is learning. The key is soaking up as much information about the present as you can so you can be a better student of the future.

The Student's Perspective

I'm a much better student as CEO than I was as a college undergrad. I have to be. The stakes are much higher now that it's no longer just about me. It's about my family, my team and their families, and the business.

There's no letting your GPA drop.

A CEO has a responsibility to learn everything about their business, the same way a homeowner knows everything about their home. It's not enough to keep it clean and tidy. You need to know the systems. Is the roof due for maintenance? Does my HVAC system need upgrading or replacing? Do I know where my gas and water shutoffs are? (In fact, I suck at all this home-based stuff—but luckily my wife has it down cold.)

You find out that stuff by learning it. It's the same in business.

It's not difficult to find the information. I read dozens of business books and other nonfiction—even fiction can sometimes help envisage where the world is heading. I listen to a couple of webinars or podcasts every week to learn how other companies approach challenges. Sometimes it's useful, sometimes it's less so—but I'll never know which unless I seek it out.

It's the same with other CEOs I'm in touch with. They were particularly useful to lean on when we were all trying to navigate the start of the pandemic. My team at ebbo™ is another source of information and knowledge, having their own specialties and backgrounds in other companies with their own processes.

I'd be a fool to ignore them, just as anyone would be a fool to reject any source of new ideas that will help them keep on top of business trends.

It's easy to get trapped in the day-to-day details and it's really difficult to keep your eyes on the bigger picture. So use the wisdom of others to help you.

The Kobe Bryant Way

Don't just look to business books to learn about business. One of the books that really opened my eyes was a biography of the basketball superstar Kobe Bryant.

Bryant was on his high-school basketball team—which I guess is no surprise, given his natural ability. The team practiced early in the morning, usually at 6 a.m., but Bryant used to get to the gym a good hour and a half before so he could work on his game by himself.

He was dedicated to overpreparation from a young age.

When he made it to the NBA, Bryant didn't let up. He was at the gym by 3:30 or 4:00 a.m. He worked out on his own, and again with his team when they arrived.

He knew that kind of schedule would have a compounding effect on his skills and his stamina.

He was right. He became one of the best players of all time.

Of course, Bryant had innate talent and ability, but his over-preparation—the thousands of hours of training beyond what his colleagues did—was what made the real difference.

Bryant's story taught me that talent isn't enough. Good enough is not good enough. Overpreparation is not an anomaly; it should be the norm.

And learning never ends. Not for an athlete and not for a business leader.

There are times, however, when no amount of preparation can give you all the information you need to make a decision. But that doesn't mean you have no resources to fall back on.

Let's look at how you can trust your gut.

CHAPTER 8

TRUST YOUR GUT

If the worst thing you have to fear is admitting "I don't know," the fear isn't worth worrying about.

That's what I reminded myself when I used to write OHS on my presentation notes.

No worry about a slipup on a spreadsheet or a poor Zoom connection comes close to the fear of emergency surgery, whether it's your own or your child's.

In business, there's rarely any real reason for fear. Once you realize that, it's easier to be confident in yourself.

Public speaking has no worries for me now. I've learned how to help an audience see through my eyes. I've also learned to lean into the emotion that sometimes leaks through (which is almost always when I'm talking about my kids). The younger me might have judged someone badly for shedding a tear during a talk; now I understand that tears are a sign of honesty, empathy, and authenticity.

They're also unavoidable, because I'm always the same person. There's no division between how I am at home and how I am in the office. I don't believe that splitting the personal and professional is healthy. It means that one or the other role you're playing is false.

It's difficult to trust yourself—and to expect others to trust you—if you're not being authentic. But you have to be able to trust yourself.

Trust you are prepared, trust you have the information you need to get your point across, and trust you can troubleshoot.

When the data is lacking, it's time to trust your gut.

Your gut is where your professional and personal persona come together. It's like a sixth sense that's based on business analytics knowledge but also on lived experience and instinct.

It's what tells you what's right or wrong, safe or risky, wise or foolish. It's what tells you which way to jump.

New Acquisition

I've already mentioned that ebbo™ acquired a new company as I was writing this book and then went through a reorganization. Meeting the new team was a revelation for me—just as meeting me was for them. They didn't quite know what to do with me, or my jokes. But even if I didn't make them laugh (and I like to think I did), I at least showed them I was personable. I wanted to take away some of the inevitable fear that comes with any acquisition, because fear can lead to a lot of mistakes and missed opportunities.

I had data to tell me what the commercial results of the acquisition would be. There was no data for its human results or its impact on the culture at the company. For that, I had to rely on my gut.

I saw very early that the leader of the new company was not like me. He interrupted his team and talked across them. He even did it to me. I had to tell him, "I'm not done with my point." I saw it too many times, and after about three months I had to have a difficult meeting with him. I told him, "This is not how it works. You can't cut people off in conversation. Your team can't cut people off."

His explanation was that his brain works fast. Well, OK, but you still have to wait for an opening. And in fact, my gut told me that it wasn't just that. It was a lack of respect for others, which is why I had to call him on it. You have to set the ground rules to protect all your employees, not just the ones you interact with every day. Crystallize your expectations sooner rather than later. If you say, "I value all the voices in the room," then act like it.

This leader was also late to meetings, which is a red line for me. I'm playful with feedback, but I still demand respect for the team's time. I'm never late, and I don't tolerate lateness in others, not my team, not my kids—and certainly not a former CEO.

It didn't have to be a big deal, so I didn't want to wait for his annual review. It's damaging to wait a whole year to air out a laundry list of how many times he interrupted or how many times he was late. If you notice a negative behavior trend, don't wait. It will rankle and cause resentment in the team. Worse still, it will green-light that behavior for everyone in the organization.

That was another thing I learned from "OHS." There's no point in wasting time because tomorrow might be too late. What if this leader's behavior loses a good team member? What if everyone starts showing up late to leadership meetings? What if everyone just stops talking at meetings, because they're not being heard? By that point, you've lost your authority and your morale, and it'll be a long hard slog to get either of them back.

Trust your gut about when to step in and when to let things ride. And trust it to allow you to communicate effectively. Show you're not afraid to talk about your kids' struggles or your own. To tell a joke that doesn't land. To take risks. That empowers a team to follow your lead and come to you honestly with their own vulnerabilities and concerns, which can be rectified before they become problems.

Data and Instinct

It can be easy to assume that following your gut is the same as following instinct. They're not the same. Your gut is instinct *informed* by data, and that data is all the knowledge you've accumulated. That's what tells me how much to risk on a new project. My gut tells me how to interact best with my team, but it's informed by the Insights Discovery personality assessment I've already mentioned. I make everyone take it to help us understand one another better.

I know I'm a red, so I can act quickly on data in front of me. I also know that a blue, in contrast, wants to mull things over and understand the reasons and theory, to go back and do more research, to see trends over time. I know I can't bulldoze a blue. I have to give him time to come slowly but firmly to a decision.

I know when I'm already jumping to the next step, he's still perfecting the plan.

Often, the blue approach is right. I know I'm not great with details. I can visualize the end, but I want others to figure out how to get there. My gut tells me they're better at that than I am.

This sort of recognition of your own strengths and those of others frees you up to follow your interests and expertise. In virtually any situation, trust that you'll do the most good doing what you're good at.

Experience and Your Gut

A CEO is a generalist. A couple of companies ago, I got put in a high-performance management rotation. The head of HR told me the rotation would give me good experience. I was reluctant. I loved the product role I had already. I had a team of thirty people, all doing great work. But HR kept coming back until finally I said yes.

My first rotation was to business development: no team, making cold calls, and cozying up to prospective clients. That was a real light-bulb moment. Nobody likes cold calls, whether they're receiving them or making them. Then it was on to client services, where I learned getting a client to even commit to a first call was a bit like getting a toddler to commit to leaving a playground. Then marketing.

Then it was back to product—but this time to run it.

HR must have seen something in me, because that rotation program gave me clarity when I eventually became CEO. I grasp how all the pieces fit together. I have knowledge of product, marketing, sourcing a client, servicing a client, coordinating, and operations. I've encountered every flavor of issue my team will encounter.

To be a good CEO is to also be a coach and mentor—and it helps when you have experienced what you're coaching. You know what can and can't be done with a given set of resources and time.

Experience is at the core of developing your gut feeling. It hones your awareness of all the moving pieces. Even if I lack data, I know my decisions are more than just guesswork.

Sometimes your gut is more reliable than the data. Years ago we needed a new head of marketing, so I asked around. Clarus's founder, who was then out of the business, recommended a friend and former coworker. He'd worked with her when she was a junior team member. She was far more high-powered now.

A solid recommendation and good experience: the data was in her favor. But as we went through the hiring process, my gut told me something was off. The half dozen people on our hiring team also had misgivings, though nothing they could put into words.

To this day, I don't know what rang my alarm bells, but I followed the data rather than my gut. I overrode the dissenting voices on the hiring team and pulled the trigger anyway.

It was clear straight away that I'd made a mistake. She didn't respond to emails. She was short with people. She wasn't a great worker. I like to highlight what's working and what isn't when I give growth-minded feedback. With her, the *isn'ts* piled up.

The day I walked into her office to let her go, she knew. Her mismatch with the company had become impossible to ignore.

The whole episode could have been avoided, so from that

point forward, I vowed to always trust my gut—even if it meant telling the founder, "It didn't work out."

That paid off in a far more positive way with another hire. We interviewed a great candidate, but she didn't fit any existing job description. My gut said, "She's going to do good work here." I had to figure out a way to get her in the building and worry later about figuring out where she reports. I was sure I was right, so I went out on a limb. I've never regretted it. What I would have regretted was letting the opportunity pass just because she didn't neatly check off the boxes.

One of the advantages of being CEO isn't only that you get to write rules in the first place. You also get to change them.

Trusting your gut is especially important when it comes time to hire your replacement. And this time will come. My own brush with death and my daughters' needs early in their lives make my time precious. I know I want to enjoy as much meaningful time with my family as possible. I know I want to bring the leadership I've learned to bigger and broader horizons.

So what do you do when you're about to sell, retire, or just move on? How do you know when a junior team member is ready for the big seat?

The Shark Tank

We've already seen that selling a company is a huge process. It's like *Shark Tank* on steroids.

It's months—years—worth of work.

Then eventually you're working with a new board. It's happened to me three times. They're into you because they see your company's growth and want it to grow more.

Some call this the honeymoon stage, when you and your new investors dance around each other, finding out what foods you both like, whether you're a sunset or sunrise type of person, whether you're football or baseball or neither.

I don't see it as a honeymoon. I call it the treadmill, because you're always on it. And this isn't a gentle walk in the park, it's a run up a mountain without a break to get a drink of water or catch your breath. You're Sisyphus, always pushing that boulder up a hill.

No one wants to buy you for a down year, or even a flat year: they want continuous progress.

What you tell them and what you do need to be aligned to build their trust—for your investors' guts to tell them they haven't made a mistake.

A CEO has little say in who ultimately buys a company, but if you've built relationships well, you can influence the process. Your board trusts your analysis and intuition, and that trust is persuasive.

After all, your board members have good guts, too. Otherwise they wouldn't be where they are.

The COVID Gut Check

Late in 2021, we held an office party. Ninety-five vaccinated employees attended. There was music, cocktails, and social interaction. If you squinted right, you could see normal life returning. I stood up on a chair and told them, "Welcome back! Thank you."

There was so much emotion packed into that thank-you.

No amount of data or experience prepared anyone in business for the pandemic. When it started, nobody knew what the next day would bring in terms of guidelines and policies, or how shutdowns would affect clients and production. There were no stable projections for getting back to business as usual.

Whatever data I could find showed that every company was doing something different. So, I took what I liked and presented a path forward to the team.

Our priorities were the health and wellness of the team. When you've been through multiple medical emergencies, that goes without saying. The team's safety was our North Star. Our identity as a company is wrapped up in the flesh and blood of the team, not the fabric of a building.

More than eighteen months later, the decision to go back to the office was also an unknown. By then, data existed that said that fully remote worked, and some companies went that route. Other companies wanted employees back five days a week, feeling the value they got from in-person interactions was worth the risk. Others decided to wait until 2022 to open their offices.

My gut said somewhere in the middle would work for us.

Sharing a physical space enhances creativity and collaboration. There's something about a whiteboard streaky with the ghosts of brainstorms or hallway conversations about kids or sports teams. These personal touch points go a long way toward building trust and cohesion. If you like your team you'll like your teamwork. Happy work makes good work.

But, as much as I see the value of face-to-face, our North Star made us proceed with precautions. As people got vaccinated, we used a hybrid model of staggered attendance—each team had office and remote days. We built in the flexibility to take on whatever the future held.

Going into the pandemic we didn't have a lot of data; coming out of it was the same. The path forward takes guts.

No Guts, No Glory

It's easier to trust your gut when you've faced the possibility that the very worst will go wrong. If you get through that, you know you can get through anything.

I still remember when the twins were born.

Dr. Death (we don't even remember his real name, he's become so wrapped in his gloomy identity) lurked in the corner of the delivery room, passing judgment on the girls' chances. Then he crept into the recovery room, where my wife was recovering from the biggest physical, mental, and emotional effort a parent can go through, even without things going wrong, and announced, "It's going to be a long haul." Michelle told her OB, "Get him out of here!"

When you're bailing water, you don't need someone poking more holes in the boat.

The bad news kept coming. Tess had to go to a new hospital in Yale for surgery. Her tiny intestines were reconnected, disconnected, reconnected again. We asked what the next steps were. The doctors weren't sure.

We kept bailing that water. We couldn't lose sight of a brighter future.

The doctor recommended Cincinnati Children's Hospital. We dug into what little data we had and found a preeminent doctor who'd done many surgeries like the one Tess needed. He said he could help her. I can't describe the amount of hope those words give a parent whose child is out of options.

We knew the doctor could only speak from his gut until surgery, but we went with him. It was a question of trusting his gut to mend Tess's literal gut.

When Tess was three, we drove to Cincinnati for a final surgery attempt.

The doctor in Cincinnati invited our Yale doctor to view the surgery. That willingness to share knowledge to help future kids was a good sign for us. It meshed with our values and signaled a collaborative personality we could work with. It made us more comfortable with our choice.

We couldn't control much else, and the control we did have led to decisions that uprooted our family and drastically changed our day-to-day existence. We would move to Cincinnati for four to six weeks. Tess had to be potty-trained before the surgery, having used an ostomy bag—an artificial gut—for the first three years of her life. We'd not only move the girls, but also our infant son. Our parents tagged along to help with the kids. It was a rotating schedule of zoos and doctors' appointments and museums and baby needs and coffee.

Lots of coffee.

The surgery worked, although there was still a moment when we didn't know if Tess would have to live her whole life attached to an ostomy bag. It turned out she didn't, but there couldn't be a starker reminder of how essential the gut is. The gut keeps us alive; if it doesn't work right, if it's injured, it can kill you.

We got another reminder when Tess had her bike accident years later and more emergency surgery. This time it was more urgent, so there was even less control for Michelle and me.

In the end, trusting our doctors worked. There was no guarantee that it would. Sometimes it doesn't. But sometimes it's the only thing you can do.

Today, we're visiting universities with the girls and helping them make their choices. They can't know everything that will follow from their decisions. All they can do is trust their guts.

No guts, no glory.

There's not a lot of time to process data in an emergency. Sometimes, you just have to lash yourself to the wheel and believe: this, too, shall pass.

The Next Chapter

Trusting your gut is not guesswork. The gut is a muscle you can improve through experience and knowledge—even the stuff that scares you.

We're taught to ignore or distrust that feeling of "Let's do it." Leaps of faith are hard, and the possibility of falling is real. But you can't go back to go forward, and sometimes you'll save a life by taking that first step.

Experience makes that step easier. So does data. If you go into a situation confident there's no challenge you and your team can't face together, you set yourself up for success. You find those solutions. You build those bridges. You fix those hearts and guts.

If you walk long enough, you realize that every valley, no matter how steep or deep its descent, starts to climb on the other side. That's the nature of valleys.

I should know. I've walked through more than my share.

So don't get distracted and discouraged by the little things. They won't be important for long. My daughters' first years may have been hell, but today they have a whole new chapter to live.

No matter how bad things get, there's always another chapter to your story.

Optimism is the only way to get through challenges in a healthy and productive way. It keeps your keel even in rough waters. I'm optimistic about my abilities to coach my team to success. I'm optimistic my kids will be healthy in the future and find the right schools. I'm optimistic about my own health and my company's health.

And, really, who do you want driving your car in the game of Life: Dr. Cincinnati or Dr. Death?

CONCLUSION

OHS. I've already explained how I wrote the three letters at the top of any presentation I did in the years after my operation to remind me that nothing I faced was as challenging as my open-heart surgery.

I don't need to do that anymore.

That's not because I no longer think about it. Every time I look in the mirror, the scar down the center of my chest reminds me of what happened and how much I have to be grateful for. In the same way, every time I watch one of the twins play sports or take her to visit a college, I'm reminded of the difficult months when they were first born.

Those aren't things I'd ever forget.

But the fact is that they've become subconscious memories now. They're a part of me and how I think—and how I present myself at work.

Being a second-chance CEO is now simply part of me. It informs every decision I make and every action I take. It's not a conscious, deliberate choice. It's a set of assumptions and principles that I never think about anymore because those assumptions and principles are part of my character.

They're the principles I've outlined in this book.

Any major medical emergency is a trauma I wouldn't wish on anyone. Going through two is more than enough for any life-time. They say that what doesn't kill you only makes you stronger. Well, I'm not dead, and the girls are still here, so I have to assume that it did make us stronger.

But I'm still not sure it was a price worth paying. If I had the choice again, I'd likely choose to learn the lessons another way.

That's why I've written this book: so you can benefit from the lessons without going through the trauma.

I prefer the latest me to the old me, naturally. He's the hus-band, father, and leader I've become, and I think he's nicer to be around. He's more patient, more empathetic, and less ego-tistical than the younger me. Maybe that's all predictable, given what I went through. What's more of a surprise, however, is that he's also more effective, more productive, and more suc-cessful in business.

It turns out you don't have to be a hard-charging, goal-ori-ented bulldog to get the most out of yourself and others. In fact, that's counterproductive for everyone—including yourself. Like surgery, business is a team game, and the team includes everyone, from the people who clean the OR to the medical experts. The surgeon you're relying on is just the person who wields the knife. They in turn rely on dozens of others to do their jobs so that the surgeon's knowledge and skill can make a positive difference.

You can't get better without trusting the surgeon, and the surgeon can't make you better without trusting their teams.

No one functions on their own.

If you want a single takeaway from this whole book, that's probably it. That's the key to achieving the humility you need to be a leader by understanding that you are not in this alone. True, you often sit in judgment of the work of others and that means you make hard decisions that piss others off, but you make them from a base of mutual respect because you depend on each other.

Some leaders feel the need to be different at work than they are at home. With me, there's no difference. I'm the same whatever the context, because to be otherwise would mean that I'm not being authentic.

Believe me, I've had a few reminders that none of us has enough time to show up as being anything other than who we are.

If you're not authentic, you can't share empathy with your team, and empathy is the key to business success. People respond well when they are understood, trusted, and empowered—and allowed to be their true selves. By being authentic, you give them permission to show up as themselves, not as some "work" persona. By being authentic to yourself and all the roles you have in life beyond the CEO's desk or the C-suite, meanwhile, you show your team how you can achieve success while achieving a balance between your work and the rest of your life.

Work isn't the be-all and end-all.

Trust me. If they were strapping you to a gurney tomorrow to go into the OR for heart surgery, you wouldn't spend today worrying about Q1 P&L or whether the sales targets for the next financial year are too optimistic.

At least I hope you wouldn't.

More likely you'd spend it with your loved ones, in quiet contemplation or sharing your fears and hopes, and offering each other emotional support. Sure, you might make a couple of calls to check on some top-level things for the welfare of your team, but if something's going to keep you awake overnight, that won't be it.

It's not always comfortable to put yourself in the hands of others, but we already do it more often than you would imagine. Every time we take a bus or eat in a restaurant, we're trusting the driver or the cook with our safety. We've gotten so comfortable with it, we don't even think about it. It's the same for the CEO. Trusting your team should be second nature.

In return, it should be second nature for them to think like you. Empower them to suggest strategies and innovations by keeping your door open and treating any suggestions with respect, even if they fade to nothing under your questioning. The more people there are in your team trying to look over the horizon, the more chance there is that you'll be prepared for whatever's out there when you get there. The more people there are who are humble enough to want to learn, the more knowledge you'll have as a business.

You set the tone and you give them permission to act like a CEO by creating an environment in which that behavior is only ever valued, never criticized. You provide an example for embracing change and never becoming so uncomfortable that it stops you from acting. You encourage them to understand and share the pain points of your business as well as to enjoy the highs. You show them how preparation—or overpreparation—is the only way to be ready for the stuff that's going to knock you off course...because you know that it will.

And when all else fails, you're the person who makes them confident to trust their gut and make the right decision, because they've seen you do it, and they've also seen you hold your hands up and say, "I failed."

They've learned that winning isn't everything, and that something going wrong at work is not necessarily a disaster. It may well be a setback, and possibly a serious one, and it can feel like a disaster—but that feeling will only last until you meet a real disaster.

That's when you find out what really matters.

And that's when you can become a second-chance CEO.

ACKNOWLEDGMENTS

I always had in my head that I wanted to write a book but I wasn't sure how to begin. As I started to crystalize the topic and found the team at Scribe, it was as if all the obstacles I had put in my own way were gone and I was free to start this amazing journey. In particular, I'd like to call out Tim Cooke, a true partner who helped me take the stories and lessons I had in my head and turn them into the book you have in your hands.

To my coworkers, bosses, board members, friends, and colleagues I have interacted with over my career: thank you for all that you have done for and with me. You have been my biggest teachers over the years and this book wouldn't have happened without you.

To my parents, Tom and Mary, and my sister, Michele: thanks for providing me with a wonderful childhood and for always supporting me and cheering me on in every stage of my life!

To my daughters, Grace and Tess: the start of your lives was rocky and unstable, but you showed the fight to survive that will serve you well as you become adults. I know you don't remember much from those early days, but the truth is that you both got a second chance to be and do whatever you want in life, which was not always guaranteed.

To my son, Tommy: while you didn't have the same medical issues as your sisters, you still had a seat on the roller coaster. Your calm demeanor and hardworking mentality will serve you well in any endeavor you take on. Some of the biggest lessons I have included in this book came from coaching you and your friends through the years.

Mom and I will be right next to all of you, rooting for and supporting you in any way we can.

CPSIA information can be obtained
at www.ICGtesting.com
Printed in the USA
BVHW020433190523
664434BV00016BA/140/J